SELFMADE

Finding the goodness and greatness within yourself

lip

Carl Foster

First published in 2012 by:

Live It Publishing
27 Old Gloucester Road
London, United Kingdom.
WC1N 3AX
www.liveitpublishing.com

Although every effort has been made to ensure the accuracy of the information, advice
and instructions contained in this book, it is sold with the understanding that neither
the author nor the publisher are giving specific diagnostic or treatment advice. Each
person has unique needs and circumstances that can present complex issues that are
beyond the scope of this book. For specific advice, the reader is advised to consult a
qualified coach or therapist.

All enquiries should be addressed to Live It Publishing.

ISBN 978-1-906954-51-2 (pbk)

It Couldn't Be Done

Edgar Guest (1919)

Somebody said that it couldn't be done,
But, he with a chuckle replied
That "maybe it couldn't," but he would be one
Who wouldn't say so till he'd tried.
So he buckled right in with the trace of a grin
On his face. If he worried he hid it.
He started to sing as he tackled the thing
That couldn't be done, and he did it.

Somebody scoffed: "Oh, you'll never do that;
At least no one has done it";
But he took off his coat and he took off his hat,
And the first thing we knew he'd begun it.
With a lift of his chin and a bit of a grin,
Without any doubting or quiddit,
He started to sing as he tackled the thing
That couldn't be done, and he did it.

There are thousands to tell you it cannot be done,
There are thousands to prophesy failure;
There are thousands to point out to you one by one,
The dangers that wait to assail you.
But just buckle it in with a bit of a grin,
Just take off your coat and go to it;
Just start to sing as you tackle the thing
That "couldn't be done," and you'll do it.

Contents

Contents

SELFMADE explained

SELFMADE explained

This book is about the challenges that one faces with oneself in order to achieve success in life. It's about overcoming temptation to quit, the temptation to be side tracked and discouraged by others, and our inner demons which laugh at us and try to keep us stuck where we are. We may have the desire, we may have the dream but do we have the will power? The power and drive to WIN.

So many big ideas today lie in the graveyard because the person who had them didn't stay on track for their implementation. They gave up at the slightest obstacle and they listened to negative self talk in their own mind. Their friends and relatives perhaps didn't support them, they got discouraged and forgot the vision that excited them in the first place.

The true winners know better. To achieve yours goals in life you must be persistent and never quit. You must express drive and determination and a burning desire to succeed. You must have a powerful belief that you can win and then surround yourself with like-minded people that will keep you on track. You can also ensure your success by unlocking the secrets to your subconscious mind, which will create a great life for you and the ones you care about. Your only challenge is you. This book will inspire you to take control of yourself and change your life for the better. This book is about remaking yourself so that you can be everything you should be.

Now let's begin...

My story

My story

I was born in the early 1970s. My early life was a struggle, including a difficult family life and battles at school due to learning difficulties. These plagued me during my school years and affected my personal development, and seemed to steal my hopes and dreams of success in life.

My mother worried about me, about how I was going to survive in this world and live a normal life. I was like other kids in having hopes and dreams, but these were cancelled out by fear.

I so much wanted to be a success at school and achieve my goals and dreams, but everything I tried met with failure and bad luck. I had to sit back and watch as everyone else progressed, leaving me behind. What could I do to turn things around for myself?

However, I did have one ace up my sleeve. I was creative and had a love for art and craft. I loved drawing and I loved music and drama. Taking part in a school play would make me feel so happy and special, as I loved being part of a team. This compensated for my failure and lack of achievement in other areas such as English and Maths. As I discovered my strengths, I also started to think about my goals.

I was also good at making things and building products using my hands or working with machines. I wanted to find a way to make a living out of these talents, since I believed that the door was closed in regards to corporate work because of my poor literacy skills.

I struggled along with no money, pursuing whatever work I could find. There didn't seem to be too many options. I lived my young life like this for many years.

Then slowly, the desire for something more and the willingness to take a chance grew in my mind; I began to see myself doing things that I had never thought possible. These feelings and thoughts developed in me thanks to some positive experiences in different jobs in the retail industry and through some training courses, plus encouragement from friends and relatives. Their strong words of wisdom helped plenty, not to mention my strong spiritual beliefs from my grandmother and my mother.

All these experiences began to give me strength of will and a positive self belief that I didn't realise I had. Despite my tough upbringing, negative self talk and hard times, I still believed in myself. I still believed I could take a chance and get out there and make something of myself. All I wanted was to be somebody. I wanted to play a part in this world! I was prepared to do what it takes and pay the price.

The price I willingly paid

The price would be to take action, studying and learning practical skills, plus learning to be patient and persistent. I began to work really hard, challenging myself in many ways: taking on jobs I knew nothing about, learning new skills through trial and error, learning on the job, seeing a positive outcome in all circumstances and seeing things through to the end. It wasn't easy at first, but it made me become stronger as a person and more creative and productive; I became a person that was never afraid to try something new.

This time was a great challenge for me that changed my life forever. I had proven the sceptics wrong. I had proven that despite my struggles in early life and growing up in a tough neighbourhood I could still survive and do well. My new hard work ethic paid off. I was always in work, or if I wasn't in full time work I would put in part time hours and study. I also did training courses to develop myself as a human being.

Despite all my learning difficulties, I discovered that I was intelligent and articulate, also good at observing and creating new ideas. I had no interest in my past concerning school; my focus was now only on my dreams. I couldn't see the obstacles that everyone else saw, I could only see what I wanted to achieve and was filled with enthusiasm and energy most of the time. I was young and eager and had a taste for life.

I went to college for a number of years and studied fashion design and business studies, and I did modelling work. I enjoyed modelling as it gave me a chance to show off all that hard work I did in the gym. I went to drama school in London for a number of years and took part in the BBC television series Grange Hill. I did Judo. I was proving to myself that there wasn't anything I couldn't do. I was self made. I could be a model, an actor, a sales person, an entrepreneur. I learned that I could do anything I pleased if I put my mind to it, and that this was possible for anyone, including someone with my learning issues.

I have learned not to focus on the current reality, but to focus on my dreams and goals; I know that nothing is impossible if you try long and hard enough. If you try hard enough, the change will come. Like anyone else I've had good times and bad times in my life, but through the change in my thinking I have learned to be happy from within and produce the results needed to improve my life for the better. What I've learned can be boiled down to this: don't live your life by fear of failure, live your life by the thought of winning.

A life saver

Sometimes people come in to our life for a reason. One day I was speaking to a delegate who was on a training course at my place of work and we talked about goals and ambitions and self achievement in overcoming adversity. She was so impressed by our conversation (and so was I) that later that day she emailed me and recommended I read a book about something called 'the law of attraction'. I took her advice and borrowed the book from my local library. This single volume changed my life for the ever.

This book showed me how to visualise success, create goals, think positive and eliminate negative self talk. It taught me why it was so important to focus only on what I wanted in life, not what I didn't want. The book taught me that the mind had power, that we are never passively thinking, and that our thoughts, whatever they are, get expressed in our reality. I learned that if you are thinking good thoughts then goodness comes into your life, and if you're thinking bad thoughts you are attracting bad things into your life. Therefore, you must be aware of your thinking and control it to your advantage. These principles are used by all successful people, consciously or unconsciously.

They think of what they want most of the time. As Earl Nightingale (creator of The Strangest Secret) famously said: "We become what we think about." I understand that if I'm feeling good and if I'm in a positive vibration I'm going to attract the good into my life. The challenge is maintaining that good feeling and not allowing outside forces to disrupt it – to stay calm and cheerful where possible. I will pass this knowledge on to my daughter when she is old enough to understand it, so she can enjoy the benefits of this secret.

I now study self help philosophy all the time, and this motivates me to focus on my goals and to think positive. I have studied the work of authors and philosophers such as Napoleon Hill (author of Think and Grow Rich), Bob Proctor, Rhonda Byrne (creator of The Secret), Earl Nightingale, and Brian Tracy. I have been strongly influenced by James Allen's classic work As a Man Thinketh, and have studied many more books and articles on self help philosophy. Through these writings I have realised that human beings all want the same thing, and that is happiness – we just have different ways of finding it. But as I've discovered, true happiness always comes from within.

From being a child who could not read or write until I was seven, I am now a SELFMADE person who can bring these ideas to many people. I have learned the keys to happiness and the benefits of a positive self belief. Now you can enjoy the benefits too. I am SELFMADE and you can be SELFMADE too.

In today's world there are millions of people going through life not believing in themselves, due to one reason or another. Some of these people are intelligent and educated and creative but are crippled by a poor self belief that is holding them from their true potential. In fear of change they stay locked into a day-to-day routine. I'm here to prove that you can make a difference and change your own life for the better by changing your self belief.

You may have overcome so many trials and tribulations already. This is a demonstration of your great power. So how can you take the next step and make your dreams come true? By applying the basic success values of faith, belief, persistence and patience. In the 1950s and 1960s the great freedom fighter Dr Martin Luther King had a dream that was so powerful it turned hatred and fear into love, joy and freedom. He was patient, he was persistent and he believed in the power of faith. He waited many years for that dream to come true and it did come true. Your dreams will come true too. By the power of your persistence you will find the answers. You are not just a being. You are a spiritual being, a life force of energy. You are a being of power and greatness. You are a part of creation and you are a creator. By the power of wisdom and faith your dreams will come true.

Chapter 1
The power of positive thinking and success

The power of positive thinking and success

We've all heard of positive thinking, but what does it actually mean? As Shakespeare said: "There is nothing either good or bad, but that thinking makes it so." There are always at least two ways to view something, and a person with a positive mind set has made a decision to be happy and cheerful, to see the good in people, their strengths and most of all to see their beauty. Yes, you are aware of the bad but your focus and interest is on the good. You have a prosperity consciousness which opens your eyes to all the good that you have and all the good that's to come. This is a very powerful mind set which reshapes the lives of millions of people all the time. It can reshape your life for the better too.

Do you see the glass half empty or half full, do you see the opportunity for happiness and prosperity in your life or do you see lack of hope and more of the same? For many, happiness and wealth seem like a distant dream. As human beings we live our lives searching for the fruitful joy of happiness, but we search for it with short term solutions which often give us more pain than happiness, leaving us feeling helpless and powerless. We feel we have no power over this pain we feel, and we live our lives without great progress, week to week and month to month.

We feel this is just the way it is, but little do we know that we are so much more than this, that we have the power to change our lives for the better. There is a great power that we are all connected to, and if we only make ourselves aware of its presence we can find a way to have true happiness and obtain the life that we want, even if we don't know what that is at this moment. So many of us go through life not thinking about what we want because we don't think we can obtain it, but little do we know that virtually any goal is possible as long as we commit to achieving it. We sometimes go through life looking for someone or something to blame for our shortfalls of happiness and success. This does nothing for us, other than create bitterness. By blaming others we are really saying we are not in control of our lives. The root to success is to take responsibility for your life. This puts you in the driving seat, and you then have the power to make changes. You must also remember that in life you can only receive what you put in.

> " Don't think of why you can't achieve something. Spend time thinking of why YOU CAN. "

Do you ever wonder why some people achieve success and happiness and others don't? To achieve success you have to know where you are going. The people who don't achieve success go through life being controlled by outside forces and situations. They are thinking 'outside in'. If we really want to make a difference in our lives we have to teach our selves to think inside out, and that means really thinking about what we want, taking time to develop ideas that will improve the quality of our life and doing what we have to do to make it happen.

This means not giving in to outside circumstances and influences. We must stay focused and be persistent in achieving our goals. I know it is difficult to learn this new mental habit after years of believing you can only have the life you were given! With a little work, old habits can and will change for you, but you must be persistent in making those changes. Only then will you start to experience the life you want.

There are only really two forces in the universe: negative and positive energy. Both forces are present in all circumstances at all times. To find true happiness and fulfilment in life you must at all times resonate with the positive energy. This means being aware of the opportunity for happiness and success in all situations, and always choosing the positive interpretation.

The people who achieve happiness in life have a definite goal in mind. They have an idea and make decisions to achieve the fulfilment of that idea. Once a decision is made it's unlikely that they will change it; they stick by their decisions through to the end, they don't give up and they don't let failure or criticism stand in their way.

If you have made up your mind that you want to achieve success and happiness, think carefully about what it is you want; write down your goals in a well-defined way. Then make a decision that you will achieve them. Think about your goal daily, visualise its achievement and take action. Goals and dreams are the stuff of life, but are worthless without action, so start today!

The power of the mind in achieving success

Remember to take control of your mind and only think of positive thoughts of achieving what you want. Be persistent and think about your goal all the time. Take control of your mind and do not allow your mind to take control of you, in thinking negative thoughts. Don't think of why you can't achieve something, spend time thinking of why you can. I know sometimes in your life you will be faced with difficult challenges and tough times; you must face these challenges head on with a positive outlook in mind.

So often we let our mind take control of us, we are plagued by negative thoughts, always thinking of what could go wrong when we should be thinking what could go right. It works both ways. We need to fill our mind with thoughts of joy and success, however our past experiences are locked deep in to our subconscious mind, and these affect current behaviour and attitude, and the experiences reappear in our thoughts and manifest in to our life, producing the same negative results. To change this, we must see and understand that we are not our minds, but that the mind is a powerful tool that we use. We must take control of our thoughts in order to feel good. This good feeling has power and then attracts more happiness into our lives; the goal is to maintain that feeling of joy and goodness.

" See the good in people, their strengths and most of all... see their beauty. "

As human beings our thoughts and feelings have power, so whatever we are thinking and feeling we will attract. If we are feeling bad or angry then we are on a negative path and will attract more of that unwanted experience, however if we are feeling good, we will attract more experiences of happiness.

The obstacles you may face on your journey to a positive and successful life

The first obstacle is always yourself. When you can overcome your habits and negative mindset that you have been enduring for years, you are then free to take a chance for success and a new life for yourself. Remember: the same actions bring the same results and new actions bring new results. Your friends and relatives and work colleagues can be negative and discourage you from achieving a positive outlook on life. Spend more time with positive people, and less with negative ones. The neighbourhood that you may live in can affect your ability to think positive and be hopeful. Think about moving to an area with a better vibe that is prosperous and has more people really doing things with their lives.

We all have greatness in us, we all are the stuff of the universe, which means we have great power, although most of us are not aware of it and never live out our true potential for happiness. All the success we want is within us; we just have to make a decision to be aware of its presence. We need to use our skills and abilities to their maximum potential and not let life pass us by. To achieve more you have to give more of yourself in all areas of your life. Make a decision to start today, take action and win the life you have always wanted. The power lies in you. You can win.

The God-like power we have in us, the power of creation

We all have a God-like ability to create. The human being has created huge buildings, cars, trucks, boats and aircraft to name a few. We have taken control of our environment and tailored it to our own needs and desires. All of this started from within one person's mind and from a goal they once had. Some of us destroy our bodies with alcohol, drugs, cigarettes and unhealthy living. It is in us to destroy ourselves. Often we follow others. We get to a point in life were the ideas dry up – there are no desires, no direction. Some of us don't know who we are, our powers, our capabilities and our strengths. We let other people and situations and circumstances rule our minds. They control our lives and destroy our dreams. However, despite these habits we can recover and get back on our feet. We need a vision, a direction, a purpose, a goal. Only then do we rediscover our God- like ability to create, and to make a life that is truly great. The evils and cruelties in this world are caused by individuals who misuse their mind power and cause pain and suffering, failing to understand the boomerang effect. What you put out must come back to you. You may defy the laws of man for a while but it is impossible to defy the laws of nature. Such individuals will pay the price with misery and sorrow in the end.

Creating ideas that will challenge you and improve the quality of your life

What is it you want? What are your current goals you have planned? Do you have any goals at all? Having read this chapter, I hope you have decided that you want to do something special with your new found knowledge. You may want to change careers and go back to college, learn a trade or improve your skills. You may decide that you want to be promoted to a higher level in your place of work, or you may already be a manager and want to be a director. You may be talented, skilled or creative in many areas and want to start your own business. You may have a product or service that is special and will improve the quality of life for many and you are trying to promote this product. You may not have the answers right now, but know you will attract the answers through your positive thinking and persistence.

You may not be happy in your relationship and want to improve it. You may be thinking about what you can do to improve it, or that your partner will give a little more love in the relationship and give a bit more of themselves too. Or you may have decided to take the serious action of walking away from a relationship and a partner that is destroying your life. You have tried over and over again with this person but they cannot make you happy. Happiness and love is what you

> " There is nothing either good or bad, but thinking it makes it so. "
>
> Shakespeare

want. You now have the courage to walk away and start a new beginning for yourself. You must stay true to what is in your heart. Live your life with love in your heart and the rest will follow. You may be single and have found the new you and would like to share that new found happiness with someone special and experience secure love and happiness from a serious relationship.

What we have learnt in this chapter...

- There are all ways at least two ways to view something and a person with a positive mind set has made a decision to be happy and cheerful, to see the good in people, their strengths and most of all to see their beauty.

- Virtually any goal is possible as long as we commit to achieving it.

- The root to success is to take responsibility for your life.

- In life you can only receive what you put in.

- To achieve success you have to know where you are going.

- We must stay focused and be persistent in achieving our goals.

- To find true happiness and fulfillment in life you must at all times resonate with the positive energy.

- Once a decision is made you must stick by it through to the end.

- Take control of your mind and do not allow your mind to take control of you.

- To find true happiness and fulfillment in life you must at all times resonate with the positive energy.

- Face challenges head on.

- We all have greatness in us.

Chapter 2
Changing
habitual ways

Changing habitual ways

Habits are incredibly important in determining our success. Our habits control our actions and have the power to override our decision making. On a conscious level we can make a decision, but will we carry it through or will we simply slip back into the comfort zone and give into our addictions to habitual ways? The answer lies with you. Have you ever wondered why you do the things you do? Why do you get the results you get?

Why is it that whatever you do, you give it your best and it always turns out the same? You may be in a situation where you know what you're doing isn't going to get you what you want but you do it anyway; you see things getting from bad to worse, but you continue none the less. Well, all this is the result of habits. A paradigm is a multitude of habits (good or bad). As human beings we don't respond to what we know, we respond to our inner behaviour patterns, our programme.

We may know something consciously but we are controlled by our subconscious programme and this dictates the life we may have, whether it is good and successful or troubled and hard. We are programmed to behave the way we do and get the results we get in life. The comfort zone gives us a faulty sense of security that so many of us fail to recognise; it acts like a smoke screen because it allows us to feel good while following bad habits. When the dust clears we're left in confusion wondering: 'How did I get here?' You got there because you followed bad habits instead of the information you hold in your conscious mind.

Overriding negative habits holding us back

When you where a baby your mind was wide open, allowing any thoughts and influences around you to be absorbed into your subconscious mind. You had little or no control at all over your thoughts. If it was a positive environment that you lived in you would take in positive influences and, likewise, if it was negative environment that you lived in you would have taken in negative influences also. The negative influences are what you need to change, as these are what are holding you back in life.

> " The winners in life have created behaviour patterns that support winning! "

Some of your behaviour patterns are inherited and some are related to your environment: where you live, who you associate with, and life's circumstances. Either way, your habitual ways and thinking control your behaviour and the actions you take. It doesn't really matter what you know mentally, because you will still take the same actions. Your conscious mind is overridden by your habits, empowered by your subconscious mind. By doing the same things over and over again, our actions become habits and can be difficult to change. A lot of people will be aware that what they are doing is wrong or incorrect but they do it anyway. They see the results in their lives going from bad to worse but they can't shake the routine behaviour pattern that is destroying their life. They want to do right and they know better but they can't get past that hypnotic routine of doing the same thing day in and day out.

However, habits can be changed by replacing them with new behaviour patterns and through repetition new habits will form and you will do things differently. This is not a walk in the park and can take time and effort to achieve, but the benefits are great. You can have a life that other people can only dream of. Your habits and behaviour patterns play a major role in your life's achievements. That's why there are some people who achieve success in almost everything they do, while others give it their best and always fall short. The winners have obtained behaviour patterns associated with winning, such as being persistent and not giving up. They are focused, they have a direct purpose or goal and they persist until they achieve their goal. They listen to good advice that is going to help them achieve their goal, they have self control and can respond to their knowledge and are not easily side tracked by outside influences. They are programmed this way, programmed to win.

As human beings we are the highest life form in terms of intelligence on the planet. Everything we need to know is within us. We know right from wrong. But can we control what is within our subconscious mind? Can we really control our inner behaviour patterns and programmes, which influence and control our results in life? When we attend our school and college all we do to retrieve the knowledge is to focus our mind and concentrate on what we are being taught. We pay attention and we listen, we repeat it and repeat it until it is stored into our subconscious mind. Our minds store the information and we draw on it to achieve success. Our only obstacle to doing right is our lack of self control: our habits and our temptations. It's never lack of knowledge, its lack of self control. It's our will power and our ability to make the right decision and carry it through. These are our challenges in achieving a fruitful life.

The habits we develop when young arise through repetition. For most of us it can be very difficult to change them. Our habits affect our relationships and the level of success we achieve at work and at school or college, and our overall happiness and well being. All the education in the world cannot change this, as the change must come from within us. An individual must first have a strong desire to break free from the inner chains that have been holding them back.

" How far we go in life is determined largely by our behaviour patterns. "

If you are not getting the results that you want in life, isn't now the time to take action and make a change? Make an adjustment in your behaviour and change your attitude, change the way you react to negative situations and challenging circumstances. Take a good look at what you are doing and think of what you could do better in order to improve your life. Sometimes just a little change can make a big difference . Start responding to what you know is right, rather than responding to negative habits and unwanted temptation that may destroy your life. Develop positive habits that will bring happiness, love and joy into your life and you will change the old programme and reprogramme yourself for a mind fit for success. You want an abundance of happiness in all areas of your life, including your job, your relationships and your health, and your overall well being. Understand that joy and happiness are a natural way to live and worth achieving.

Recovering from adversity

As human beings we make mistakes. We give into our emotions, our feelings of temptation and our anger and frustrations. We react; we mess up; we lose control. When the damage is done we sometimes sit down and blame ourselves or we blame others, not understanding that it is sometimes natural to give in to our constant challenges. When we are born we develop negative behaviour due to our environment or genetic inheritance, but the good news is that human beings are very resilient and can rise above this. In most cases we can grow as an individual and become a better person. We learn to control ourselves and not give in to our negative feelings, and this self-control stops us from taking negative action every time we feel threatened. Although in life we sometimes fall down, we have the power and greatness to rise up and recover from our challenges. We have the ability to come back stronger than ever. It is all in the power of our minds; use this power and build the life you want. Erase your negative thoughts and actions and win the life you want.

Habitual habits and self image

Are your habitual ways getting you down? Do you desire a healthier body? So many of us have a poor self image. The idea of having the body we want is inconceivable, it seems. But just like anything else, if you put good effort into your health and well being, you must get results.

If you desire a healthier body and are having problems with weight loss, your current life style may be a contributing factor. You may have fallen into the pattern of bad eating habits. Some people may say: "I only have one large meal a day" and therefore feel that should equal a small waist line. In fact, one large meal a day will most likely increase weight, because your body is registering famine and so will store the food you eat. Snacking can be another habit to increase weight gain.

Habits that can contribute to weight gain:

• Snacking (eating high calorie snacks throughout the day);
• Comfort eating (eating comfort foods for happiness to replace low self-esteem);
• Late night eating (consuming more calories than you are burning);
• Non active life style (lack of fitness activity); and
• Poor diet (non constructive eating habits)

If you seriously want to lose weight and get in shape you can, but your habits are the key. Most people's appearance indicates their life style: if you're a social drinker and a smoker you will have the appearance of a drinker and a smoker. If you live on fast foods or have a high calorie diet, it will show in your appearance.

The same applies if your lifestyle consists of playing golf or tennis on the weekends or visiting the gym three times a week or swimming. All of these activities will affect your health and physical appearance for the better. We wear our lifestyles on our sleeves.

Whatever lifestyle you have, it will affect your physical well being in one way or another. In order to lose weight and have the body you desire you have to first make a definite decision to lose weight and start planning. You need to look at your current life style. What is it that you eat regularly? How often do you eat?

> **" Your habits and behaviour patterns play a major role in your life's achievements. "**

The challenges for most people who want to lose weight are their habits and a mindset that may tell them they can't have the body they want. Other factors can be low self esteem and comfort eating. They get into a routine of eating for a certain reason or at a certain time of the day. Whatever the reason, the fact is this life style isn't getting them the results that they want and now it's become a way of life. A person may decide to join the gym or go on a diet and try to change their lifestyle, but to overcome ingrained negative health habits is a challenge. We've lived this way for so long that it becomes painful to change it. However, it can be changed, and the individual has to make a decision that they want to lose weight and have the body they desire.

To make the change and start moving forward, action is required.

You could start today and enquire about local fitness classes and gyms in your area. Have your gym put together a fitness plan for you, after clearing it first with your doctor. Put together a healthy and alanced diet using a nutritionist. Take up sports and leisurely activities that you enjoy and love. As you incorporate these activities into your daily schedule they will become a way of life. For those who do not like the gym or other vigorous physical activity, you will at least need to be more active and eat less and have a healthier low fat diet. You will need to walk more (take the stairs instead of the lift, get off the bus a few stops early), have regular meals at set times, and eliminate the habits of having one large meal per day, snacking and comfort eating. However, before you take any physical action you should always seek medical advice from your doctor. Make sure you are fit and well enough to take on a more physical lifestyle. Whatever your efforts in obtaining the physical appearance you desire, it will be the result of your life style. How we live shows in our physical appearance.

So many of us want the body of our dreams but fail to achieve it. Because of our self doubt, we don't believe it is possible, but once you make a decision and start planning it will become a reality. Get confirmation from your doctor that you are fit enough to take on physical activity and start living an active and healthy life. It is amazing when you see your physical body change and gradually transform your image as you desire it to be! Once it becomes a way of life you will love your new, healthy you and not have to work so hard at being motivated. You will surprise yourself and others.

Build habits that give you the life you want

When a person has made up their mind that they are going to have the life they want, no one can stop them. They have made a decision from within, and what is true within becomes true without. They are like a missile heading towards its target. This individual will use all resources available to succeed in achieving their goal. Once you have achieved total control of your habits through repetition of your chosen behaviour patterns, your result will look something like this: you will be able to naturally give 100% to your work and career; in your relationships to partner, family and friend;, and to your health and fitness.

Success is abundance in all areas of life. You are now happy at work, you are now happy in your home with your partner, you are now happy with family and friends; your health and well being is looked after, you are now fit and well enough to be more active in your life. All of this is achieved by a strong will and commitment to achieve more. It requires repetition of productive behaviour in all areas of life. This level of achievement requires dedication, and only the very few do this naturally. But with good practice and commitment it can be achieved by any individual. How far we go in life is determined largely by our behaviour patterns, as it is these which determine the actions we naturally take. If your habits are holding you back from the life you want you must take action to make the necessary changes in your behaviour.

What we have learnt in this chapter...

- Habits can control our lives and they have the power to override our conscious decision making.

- Habits have the power to control our thoughts and actions.

- In order to change our lives we must change our habits.

- A paradigm is a multitude of habits (good or bad) formed in our subconscious mind.

- As human beings we don't always respond to what we know; some times we respond to our behavior patterns, our program, our paradigms.

- When you were a baby your mind was wide open allowing any thoughts and influences around you to be absorbed into your subconscious mind, you may have had little or no control at all over this.

- Habits can be changed by replacing them with new behavior patterns.

- It requires repetition for new habits to be formed.

Chapter 3
The great law –
the law of attraction

The great law –
the law of attraction

We live in a world where everything is in line with logic. We trust in what we see, touch, smell, taste and hear. We believe in practical things with practical explanations. We question things that we have no logical explanations for. Such things we classify as spiritual or invisible energy. Anything that has no practical explanation, or that we can't see, is ridiculed as madness or craziness. This is how most of us think today. This is part of the comfort zone and anything with no physical or practical explanation tends to put us in fear.

The law of attraction is a universal law, the law of like attracts like. The law of attraction is essentially the vibration of energy. The energy of the universe vibrates and it creates a frequency of positive and negative energy. Everything in the universe is energy, our body is energy, and the world we live in is energy. The stars, the planets and rocks are all energy. Everything in the universe is energy. And this energy vibrates and emits a frequency, attracting things of a similar frequency to you. The very thoughts that go on in your mind have a frequency and are made of energy, and as each energy force is attracted to like energy, negative energy is attracted to negative energy and positive energy is attracted to positive energy.

The very thoughts that go on in your mind are made of energy and when you are thinking a thought you attract the energy that is on the same frequency with that thought, be it negative or positive energy. You are what you think about. If you're thinking negative thoughts the law of attraction then picks up your vibrations and you will attract negative situations into your life, and if you are thinking positive thoughts you will attract positive situations into your life. The energy you attract is in harmony with your thoughts, and this power is not concerned if the energy is good energy or bad energy. You will attract in relation to what is in your mind.

This great law not only responds to your thoughts but it also responds to your feelings. If you are feeling good you're in harmony with positive energy, and you will attract more positive things that are in harmony with that positive energy; if you're feeling bad you will attract more negative things that are in harmony with that negative energy. It's that simple. It's very important to feel good and harmonious and joyous, as these feelings of joy will then attract more great feelings.

> " Your thoughts are made of energy
> and have a frequency. "

It is very important to take control of your mind and direct it to what ends you desire to avoid attracting what you don't want. Everything that's coming to you, you are attracting, and it is in perfect relation to your thoughts and feelings. You may not have realised that your emotions have this great power. The law of attraction is a universal law just like gravity: it never fails, working all the time and responding to your vibrations and your thoughts. We can change our vibrations to attract positive energy or to attract negative energy. Now that you are aware of these principles you can use them to your advantage and attract the good that you want in to your life. Think of love, joy, peace, wealth and happiness and expand on these thoughts. Focus on how good it is and how good it's going to get. Think, feel, vibrate and attract!

Using the law of attraction to your advantage

You may ask why doesn't everybody use this great law to their advantage and live the great life? Well, most of us are plagued with negative thoughts of doubts and fears. We talk about what we don't like. We are distracted by things that are going on all around us. We have made it a habit to think that way. We have made it a habit to think about our worries and fears. We are constantly focusing on our current problems, thus attracting more problems. We may be influenced by family, friends and colleagues at work, who worry about problems and no solutions. We listen to the media, the local news informing us of how bad things are and how bad it is going to get. Very few of us are focused on what we want, our hopes and dreams. It can be very hard for a person who has experienced pain, failure and sadness all their life to suddenly believe that they have some influence over what is going on in their life. We believe the nightmare that is in front of us, and we forget the dream.

You may have experienced a moment in your life when you had a good idea or a solution to a problem, and you felt great and empowered.

Then suddenly a person or an individual may have said it's not possible, you can't do it. They try to tell you all the reasons why it cannot work. Suddenly you feel that power within you disappear; those negative words bring you back down. These are the challenges that make the law of attraction a difficult if not impossible habit for some of us to form and use to our advantage. We get discouraged by other people's words and their way of thinking, or our own doubts and fears.

> " Negative energy attracts negative energy. Positive energy attracts positive energy. "

To truly use the law of attraction to your advantage, you must change your way of thinking. You must be in a state of joy. If you are naturally influenced by other people and the things going on in your life this may be the area to work on. Some inner work and training may be required to change your mindset and get you on the road of thinking positive and developing thoughts of happiness and prosperity. For a person to turn their life around it is good to start being grateful for what you have, to be assertive and observant and become aware of the good you already have achieved. So many times we are stressed, angered and distracted by the negative things going on around us that we cannot see the love and joy we have in our lives. The problems blind us to the greater good we already have. We just need to be aware of the good we have and then by the law of attraction we will attract more good into our lives. Stay calm and collected, be cheerful, kind and loving to others. Learn to live this way and attract goodness into your life. By practising this way of life over and over again it will then form as a habit. Surround yourself with positive people. If you are in a negative mind set you will then attract more negative people into your life and this will take you backwards. You must be selective with your company and your surroundings, as your environment can and will affect your mood.

The feelings of positive and negative energy

Energy is a powerful thing, a thing that we can almost see and feel. We are able to 'see' energy when it is expressed in the form of a human being. When a person walks in a room, immediately you can feel the energy they are transmitting. Before they come into view you can pick up a feeling of their energy force, be it positive or a negative. A negative energy force is easy to recognise as it sets up feelings of tension, or that something is brewing. A person transmitting negative energy need not say much as their vibrations are transmitted through all they come into contact with, creating like minded negative situations that are on the same frequency as them. A negative mind creates worry and fear, which make you feel stressed and crippled. You are programmed to feel helpless, and in this state your abilities to be creative in thinking of solutions are much hampered. In contrast, a person transmitting positive energy brings joy and laughter to the party. They bring reassurance and joy. They think of solutions to any problem or situation, and they attract many people like a magnet. People want to be around a person like this simply because they make them feel good. A positive person transmits positive energy and brings the light of happiness and joy into everything that they come into contact with. Suddenly you feel you have plenty when in contact with a positive life force of energy. When we think from a positive point of view we see solutions not problems. Be aware of your feelings and see the bright side of life and attract the beauty that life has to offer you.

We are energy

So many times human beings get it wrong. We think the human body is who we are. Yet your body is just your host. Your body is expression, almost like a dumb terminal controlled by your mind, feelings and thoughts, yet whatever your thoughts or feelings are, they are expressed through your body. Consider for example the host of a television channel. People watching associate the host as the channel, they ignore the fact that there's a director, a script writer, a producer, organisers, production team and so on. Well, the same applies with a person: the body is an expression of your mind and soul: you have a conscious mind, a subconscious mind and a spirit and soul. The real you is energy; a life force of energy. Everything in the universe is energy. The body is expression, an extension of who you are. It is made up of atoms and cells all moving in harmony with your thoughts and feelings. Energy is not created or destroyed, energy has always been. We are all made up of energy, which means we possess great power and can attract things into our life through our feelings and thoughts.

Our many levels

As human beings, we operate on four levels:

    1. Our physical body – atoms, energy, water, mass of molecules vibrating at a high speed. Our body is not solid as it appears; it is a mass of energy.

2. Our conscious mind – energy

3. Our subconscious mind - energy

4. Our spirit/Soul the inner core – energy life force (You)

Energy and the law of attraction: a summary

- **Energy changes form**. Energy can take on the form of a star/sun, a moon,a planet, a plant, a piece of rock or flesh and blood. It can take on the form of a human being. Energy is everything.
- **Energy vibrates**. Positive energy vibrates differently to negative energy and energy attracts like energy. Positive energy attracts positive energy and negative energy attracts negative energy.
- **Everything that is negative attracts negative energy** and everything that is positive attracts positive energy, which is why it is so important to stay in that positive vibration, inviting all the good stuff to come into your life and making your life rich with love, joy and happiness.

You're a spirit, a soul in a physical body, travelling through time and space. You are energy and you can vibrate in a positive or negative vibration, and you control your vibrations by your thoughts and feelings. You have attracted everything in your life and you have attracted these things through the thoughts in your mind, which affect your feelings. This includes your family, friends, your home, your place of work and your car. Everything flows in harmony with your vibrations. You have called them into your life by your thoughts, feelings and vibrations.

What we have learnt in this chapter...

- Everything in the universe is energy and like energy attracts like energy.

- Positive energy attracts positive situations and circumstances and negative energy attracts the negative situations of life.

- We become what we think about.

- If we think negative thoughts we attract negative things into our life.

- It is important to think positive thoughts.

- Focus on love, joy and happiness.

- This great law responds to our thoughts and also to our feelings.

- If you are feeling good you are in harmony with positive energy and will attract good into your life.

- If you're feeling bad you're in harmony with negative energy and will attract negative energy into your life.

- You are like a magnet attracting positive and negative forces.

- It is very important to take control of your mind and focus on what you desire in order to avoid attracting what you don't want.

- Everything that is coming into your life, you have attracted to you.

- The formula is simple...Think, feel, vibrate!

Chapter 4
The art of creative visualisation

The art of creative visualisation

Creative visualisation is the great power of the mind that allows us to 'see' things before they actually happen. Have you ever thought to yourself: "I want to do something big or something special, but I just can't see how it's going to manifest?" Many people have an idea that they want to create something big, some sort of achievement, but they just can't seem to picture it in their mind. To really achieve what you want you must start at the core, you must believe it is possible. This is where visualisation comes in to play. Visualisation is a power that all successful people use to get what they want out of life. They actually see themselves obtaining success before they've achieved it. This reinforces their belief that they can have it. See yourself in that new job, see yourself in a happy and fruitful relationship and a happy family life, and you will start to believe it's possible and attract it into your life.

Visualisation is so powerful because if you can actually see something in your mind you will start to believe it. Visualise an image in your mind over and over again and you will start to get passionate and emotional with it. You will start to believe it's possible and that belief is the key, the trigger to making it happen. Over time, what you are visualising becomes natural to you, as if it has already happened.

It is so natural for us to visualise what we don't want when we see the current problem in front of us. We dwell on memories of past results and we then set our self imposed limitations which hold us back. And what happens? Instead of a breakthrough we just get more of the same. So many of us go through life never really testing our capabilities and living the life we want because we don't think it's possible. It so important to understand that things don't just happen to us, that we can take responsibility for ourselves and improve our lives. If you are constantly experiencing a problem, this is an indication that something is wrong inside. Your life is an expression of what is going on inside your mind, specifically the habits and the images you have deep in your subconscious mind.

> " Whatever you visualise repeatedly will materialise into your reality. Focus only on the positive and on improving the quality of your life. "

Most people in life misuse the power of visualisation. They use it not to create the desired life, but to replay past events and to re-create more of the same. They are plagued by the everyday things that they don't want, and the images of these things fill their minds. If you are constantly worrying or if you are living in fear you may be visualising images that may change your life for the worst. Remember, whatever you visualise long enough will materialise into your reality. The good news is that once you become aware of this, you can be careful about the images you are filling your mind with. It may take some practice to get use to it, for this to become a habit, but once mastered and used effectively it can change your life for the better. Successful people use these techniques all the time. They visualise their goals and programme their minds to push them into action to make it happen. Suddenly they are attracting all the resources needed to make their vision come true. For the most part, most successful people are not even aware of what they're doing, as positive visualisation is just a habit. They naturally visualise the things that they want as they have a prosperity consciousness, and focus only on opportunity and improving the quality of their life.

The power of visualisation doesn't discriminate against good or bad images in the mind. If you're thinking good positive thoughts most of the time you're allowing that good to come into your life, and if you're thinking negative thoughts then you're sowing the seeds for negative stuff to manifest in your life. The visualising power simply converts the images you hold in your mind into reality.

" Successful people visualise themselves being successful before they've actually achieved it. "

Now you may start to understand how, if used the right way, visualisation can be a major tool to making your dreams come true. You will start to see your dreams expressed in an uncanny way; it can be scary and exciting all at the same time. When you're thinking negatively it's hard to notice that the visualisation is coming from you as most people visualise similar situations. But when you start to visualise your goals long enough for them to manifest you will surely notice the difference. And you will be more than pleased.

To help you with your visualisation, make a vision board with pictures of a place or a thing that you want: it could be a car, a nice home, a loving relationship; the images should relate to your vision of what you want. Look at your vision board every day. You can also add inspiring music of your choice to give an emotional effect to your visions. The emotions will make it work faster for you. You will swing into action. Over time you will find yourself attracting people and places and the circumstances to make it happen. If you look into your past you may realise that similar circumstances may have all ready manifested this way, but you weren't aware of it.

Visualisation is a technique used world over by companies and organisations. They visualise their goals and objectives. Most organisations visualise how they want their company to be, and what sort of customers they are targeting. They hold meetings to share their vision with employees, they advertise and market to inform the customer of their vision, so everyone involved can see where they are going. This same power can be used as an effective way of achieving your goals and improving your life.

I reiterate that that your limitations are self imposed and drawn from past and current events. You look at your school results, your medical results, your current job, friendships, relationships and you believe this is it, this is my life, this who I am – and of course this isn't

> " Anything you want in life is
> possible. If you can see it
> on the screen of your
> mind it is possible to achieve! "

true. The current results are a product of past thought and past actions and you can change your life right now. Visualise your future and direct your thoughts to what you want and attract it in to your life. To achieve success you must have direction, you must know where you're going. There will be times when you feel like giving up, but you must be persistent in your visualising and in time your current circumstances will change accordingly, matching up to your goals and your vision.

Change the image you have of yourself and change your life

If you would like to be more assertive, more confident and more successful, visualise the person that you would like to be, visualise your success as if it's already here. When you visualise the things you want, you see it as if it's already accomplished. This puts you in a good mood, the mood of success. You start to feel creative, you start to create ideas and think of possibilities, solutions and resources. Everything starts in the mind and is expressed through our body, our behaviour and our actions. Stay positive and visualise the good that you want in life and if you do this often enough it will materialise into your reality, I promise.

You can achieve anything if you put your mind in to it! As human beings we have great power and the capability to achieve anything, and we have proven this each century, and will continue to do so. When you see a person who is successful, don't envy, hate or ignore them, because that person's success is your confirmation that you can do the same, maybe even better. Their success is your clarity that you can achieve your goal; you can achieve your dreams. After all, we all possess this great power of visualisation which can see our dreams implemented. All successful people have proven that it is possible to achieve the things we want in life. Let their success prove to you that your dreams are possible too. And learn from them and take action and make it happen. Anything you want in life is possible if you can see it on the screen of your mind it is it is possible!

What we have learnt in this chapter...

- Our ability to visualize is one of the greatest powers of the mind and creative thinking.

- Creative visualization allows a person to see events before they happen.

- Visualization is powerful because if you can see what you want in your mind you will start to believe it's possible.

- Belief has power.

- The power of visualization doesn't discriminate against good or bad images held in the mind.

- Your mind will manifest whatever images you create in your mind into your life.

- Practice visualizing beautiful images in your mind.

- Through repetition, you will learn to visualize the images that you want and manifest these

Chapter 5
The conscious and the subconscious mind

The conscious and the subconscious mind

The subconscious mind is the great power that controls almost everything in your life. It has power over your thinking, your logic, and your belief systems. More often than not your subconscious mind is in conflict with your conscious mind due to the fact that you can think something on a conscious level but your subconscious mind will actually decide whether you will do it or not. If it goes against what you believe in your subconscious programme, it may be difficult to achieve. That's why most people never really live out their true desires in life, because they are controlled by their subconscious mind, which is keeping them right where they are.

Your mind's power is a combination of your conscious and subconscious mind. Your feelings and thoughts are expressed through the physical instrument called your body, and what is in must come out. The life we live is simply the expression of our thoughts. However, so many times we use our mental powers to our disadvantage by reacting to outside circumstances, events and situations.

We focus on this problem and that problem; we do this or that as part of our habitual way of thinking. We see only the problem and no solutions. As we lock in to this way of thinking we achieve more of the same results. It's a vicious circle which keeps us where we are. We are not aware that we are actually doing it to ourselves. We are constantly feeding our subconscious mind with these negative thoughts of our problems, over and over again. By indulging in this thinking, we are simply programming ourselves to attract more of the same. Whatever you feed your mind must eventually be expressed.

However, we can use this situation to our benefit by thinking about the things we desire. We must first be aware of ourselves, who we are as a person and what it is we want. Most of us forget about what we want or we may not know what we want as we are consumed by our day to day problems and our negative way of thinking. But if we become self aware we can start to resonate with the positive, and this takes us away from our current circumstances and allows us to find that genius side to our personality which all humans have. We then work with our creative mind to find ideas and solutions and work towards a happier life. We must start to use our belief systems and start to understand that what we focus on and believe in will come true in our real world. What starts in the mind must eventually be revealed.

Why we fail and our subconscious mind

Every human being that enters the world is programmed in one way or another due to our genetics and our surroundings, and through the environment that we lived in as a child.

As we grow older we add to these programmes, some of which serve us well, and others that don't. Life can pass us by if we don't realise the negative dominant programme that has a grip on us. This programme controls everything: our thinking, our thoughts and actions, all of which make it a challenge to achieve success. This unwanted programme comes from our subconscious mind and is like a smoke screen holding us back.

Consciously we can decide to improve, but subconsciously the old programme will hold us back as we are programmed and controlled by the subconscious mind to stay where we are. That's why most people find it so hard to make a change in their life. They read the books, they attend the class and the so called life changing seminars, the information and the knowledge is there but they are not using the information because their actions and behaviour are being controlled by their subconscious mind.

But this is not to say that a human being should give up on their dreams and indulge in procrastination; it means that an individual must dig deep and take action in order to achieve success. You must focus on your goals every day by the use of positive affirmations and vision boards and creating new habits that will lead you to success, and which will re-programme your subconscious mind. Surround yourself with positive people who have achieved what you want to achieve in life and change your mindset for the better. Never give up on your dreams. Hold love and desire in your heart and give more of yourself in everything you do and get more out of this life you have been given.

In order to achieve a more fruitful life you must set your goals and be persistent and see them through to the end. Goals give a human being power and direction. Write them down. Focus on them daily and believe in them. Use the power of the law of attraction – think, feel and attract.

> " Your subconscious mind has power over your thinking, your logic and your belief systems. "

The conscious mind has control over the information it allows into our awareness. This information is then fed to the subconscious mind, which is a massive source of potential power, shaping your behaviour and life. You are the gate keeper of your subconscious mind and whatever you allow into it must manifest, be it good or bad. You decide on what you want to bring in to your life; the subconscious mind has no control over what is fed into it. It will allow any information through and accept it, be it negative or positive. Therefore, in order to obtain the good that you desire, you must feed your subconscious mind positive fruitful thoughts and over a period of time you will see the benefits and improvements in your life. But if you are allowing negative thoughts into your subconscious mind by outside situations or negative thinking this will influence your subconscious mind and affect your results. We all attract situations that are on par with our conscious feelings and thoughts, and this power is expressed from our subconscious mind. It is only concerned with what you think and feel. To put it another way, your conscious mind is like the doors to a great mansion, only allowing invited guests to enter. In order to feel good and attract happiness and wealth, you must think and focus on happiness and wealth. You must take control of your thoughts and decide on what you are going to focus on, because whatever you focus on you will attract.

Negative thoughts can be formed from the environment that you live in – from childhood experiences, from your community and from family and friends. Although your family and friends care about you and love you, they can unconsciously or consciously hold you back from achieving success and fulfilling your true potential. You may have a goal to apply for a job or start up a business. You've made up your mind you feel great... and then a friend or a relative begins to inform you of all the problems in achieving your goal, telling you what can go wrong.

> " You must focus on your goals every day by using positive affirmations and vision boards. "

Before you hear these words you felt fulfilled and ready to take action on your goal, and suddenly these negative words from someone close to you bring you down. You start to feel fear, doubt and uncertainty. You must not allow that to happen. You must continue to feed your mind positive images of success. Visualise your goal and feed that image into your subconscious mind and turn it in to reality. In life we will often experience situations that may distract us from our goal. It is our job to stay focused and on track.

We are not the mind. The mind is something that we have. It's our aid. The mind is our support mechanism, our guide. It gives us thoughts, ideas and direction. It feeds information, it attracts things to us. We must take responsibility for our mind and feed it with the good we want. Our body is our expression of the mind. Whatever is going on in the mind is expressed through the body. If the mind is in joy and happiness, you will see that joy and happiness expressed through the body. You will see health and well being in a happy soul. With that joy comes power and energy. That power is the power of creation. You will not feel tired when you're in a creative mode.

However, if the mind contains anger, sadness or hate, that is also expressed in the body. You will see ill health, pain, stress and tiredness. Stress in the body can cause sickness and disease. This is the result of negative thoughts and emotions. You can never be happy in life with hate in your heart.

To change this state of being, turn that negative energy and emotion into love, joy and happiness. Start to see the good in your life and see the good in yourself and the people in your life. See the good in human beings. Your subconscious mind is so powerful that it manifests the things that you think about. What are you feeding your mind? Think about it carefully because it will come true. Think peace, joy, love and happiness.

Can words really hurt?

It is said to small children that *sticks and stones can break my bones but words can never harm me*. Is it true that words can never harm? Negative words, if fed to the conscious mind, may pass through to the subconscious and may manifest in your life. Remember, the mind isn't stagnant or stationary. Mind is movement, it is energy. The information that words bring can make you feel a certain way, and that feeling influences your thoughts and actions. In young children it is very serious and important what is fed into their minds.

A young child who is constantly being put down and shouted at by a parent or loved one may feel they cannot do anything right. The child may feel stupid, inferior, unloved and unimportant. It can and will affect them for some time, sometimes for life. Another child, on the other hand, may be loved and encouraged, and their parents constantly tell them that they have greatness in them, that they are good and they will have a great life and that life is easy and rewarding. It is most likely that child will be a success, because they have been told from the start that they have greatness in them. Feed the child the idea of success and the child will go in search of it.

Your mind is like a powerful computer storing information. What do you feed your subconscious mind? What are you exposed to everyday of your life? Do you spend your time surrounded by people with big ideas who enjoy life and make the most of it, or are you surrounded by people who see the glass half empty? What people say to you can be so powerful; their words can pick you up or pull you down, if you let them. It's up to you. You're in the driving seat of your life.

> " Use your creative mind to find ideas and solutions that move you towards a happier life. "

For true happiness and joy to manifest we must be particular, we must be choosy and fussy about what we allow to enter into our mind and influence our thinking. Sometimes we have no choice over the environment we live in, but we do have a choice over what we allow to enter our subconscious mind.

> " You are the gate keeper of your subconscious mind. Whatever you allow into your subconscious mind must manifest, be it good or bad. "

What type of music do you listen to? What type of movies do you watch? All of this has an effect on your feelings and your mind. How is this material making you feel when exposed to it? Does the music you listen to make you feel good, do the movies and books you read make you feel good? Are you feeling up lifted and inspired? What information are you receiving and what is it telling you? Is it positive information that will improve your life and make you a better person? Or is it putting you in a negative mental state? If it is making you angry, think of the implications. Think of what that will do to your life and the people around you. Anger is negative energy and should not be allowed to fester in your mind. You must expose your mind to positive and constructive information.

Express positive emotions and believe in yourself and believe in your dreams. You must believe. You can be happy. You can win. Believe and it will come true. Don't entertain negative talk from others or be exposed to a negative environment. Don't allow yourself to be easily influenced by destructive people. Be strong in your thinking and stay positive. In influencing the subconscious mind to serve you it is important to be aware of the day to day emotions you feel – are they happy, confident, cheerful emotions or are they emotions of fear and worry? Are you an angry person?

Below are the seven positive emotions that will lead you to success and happiness, plus the seven deadly emotions you must avoid by thinking positively and maintaining control over your thoughts:

1. **Desire**
2. **Faith**
3. **Love**
4. **Passion**
5. **Enthusiasm**
6. **Hope**
7. **Happiness**

These seven positive emotions will bring you joy and happiness in life and to the people you love. Feel joy and happiness and love!

The seven negative emotions to avoid:

1. **Fear**
2. **Jealousy**
3. **Hatred**

4. Revenge

5. Greed

6. Superstition

7. Anger

These seven are deadly and will destroy your life if left to manifest in the subconscious mind, so if you are feeling any of these, do something about it! Try to replace them every minute with more rewarding and loving emotions.

When you are feeling good the answers to any troubles or challenges in life will come in to your mind, the solutions will flash into your consciousness one by one. You will then experience the power of creation as you become clearly aware of the solutions to any problem, receiving the right ideas to move forward. But when you are feeling low you will see all the obstacles, all the reasons why it's not possible. Yet all things are possible to those who believe. By understanding these principles, you will then use them to your advantage and maintain a sense of joy and love in your consciousness at all times. Use the knowledge of this book, take control over that powerful mind that all humans have been granted and change your life for the better and turn those dreams of yours into a reality.

What we have learnt in this chapter...

- Due to our genetics, our surroundings and the environment that we lived in as a child, every individual is programmed in one way or another.

- We are not the mind.

- The mind is something that we have, and it's our aid.

- The mind is our support mechanism - our guide.

- The mind gives us thoughts ideas and direction.

- The mind finds information and the answers to our problems.

- You are in charge of your mind.

- We must take responsibility for our mind and feed it with the good we want.

- Our body is our expression of the mind.

- Whatever is going on in the mind is expressed through the body and becomes our reality - our life.

- Your subconscious mind manifests the things that you think about.

- Turn negative energy and emotion into love, joy and happiness.

- Your conscious mind is like the doors to a great mansion only allowing invited guests to enter!

Chapter 6
Attitude of gratitude

Attitude of gratitude

Gratitude is the attitude of only seeing the good in your life and the good to come. Do you see the good in your life, the richness? Or do you find yourself complaining and grumbling about what you don't have? Do you live an existence of blame and regret or are you constantly complaining, speaking of lack, limitation and want?

Ungrateful behaviour leads to anger, sadness and hate, and these negative emotional states produce lovelessness, lack of friendships, lack of money and ill health. To turn your life around, dig deep and see the riches in your life. You may not seem to have much right now, but when you change your attitude and start to praise the good that you have you will begin to feel better and you will attract more. You may become aware of the opportunity for love, the opportunity for success in your current job, be the best you can be and achieve more. The opportunities you want may be right in front of you: reach out and grab them and make that change in your life that will bring you happiness and joy.

Even if you're just happy to be alive and able to make choices in your life, this small gratitude can bring joy and happiness. A good attitude allows you to grow. This positive energy brings more good into your life and gives you a chance to build bigger achievements that bring joy and happiness into your life again and again. Every morning give thanks for what you have: your family, friends, relatives, good health and well being, your job. You will get more when you start to open your eyes and appreciate what you have. When you start to be grateful you will soon realise that you have good in your life. You are alive and in a position to make decisions that can change your life and the people in it for the better. The power of gratitude will open your awareness into seeing opportunity and not the lack of it. When you do a stocktake of your achievements, suddenly you see that you have the foundations to achieve an even bigger goal than what you thought was possible. You will start to see that you have great friends that will help you when you cry for help, you see that you do have love in your life, you notice that people care about you and love you; you start to see what's important. A grateful attitude hooks you up to your source of supply, both in terms of success and love. When you are grateful for what you have, you will open up yourself to achieving more.

> " The power of gratitude will open your awareness to seeing opportunity as opposed to limitations. "

Don't spend your time living a life of blame and regret and anger, because that attitude will not help you move forward in life. Ungratefulness only leads to sadness. Live a life of gratitude. Be grateful that whatever you've been through you have come out of it alive and can rebuild your foundations again. Be grateful to those who notice your inner joy, see and understand that you do have love in your life.

If you have given up and are giving little or no effort in your life, it's like being on a ship with no control over where it is going; you're just aboard for the ride, your life isn't in your hands. To have the life you want you have to put in that level of effort. Before you walk away from your current job, your current relationship or your family and friends, ask yourself: is there really nothing more you can give to turn it around and achieve the riches you deserve? For most of us we always feel the grass is greener on the other side, only to find that it's not. Before walking away from any situation in life, you must be sure that you have fully assessed that you are getting the most out of it, and to do so you have to give it your best. Only then you can know if it is worth your while investing your time and effort into it.

> " Live your life with an attitude of gratitude and see wealth in every context of your life. "

It's a natural state of mind for a human being to be grateful for their achievements but still feel dissatisfied in other areas of their life. Dissatisfaction indicates our need to grow and expand. Due to dissatisfaction we have created a life that is more comfortable than earlier generations could ever have imagined. In 1908, Henry Ford created his model T motor car. The success of the model T continued through to 1927, bringing a transport revolution that replaced the horse and carriage and made life more comfortable for millions.

In 1903, the Wright brothers, who were simple bicycle mechanics, turned their eyes upwards and dreamed of being the first people to fly. For centuries people had dreamed of flying, and the Wright brothers turned the fantasy into reality when, after years of trial and error, they created the first aeroplane. Many people doubted them because it was thought illogical for anything heavier than air to fly. But they proved the critics wrong and today we can relax and enjoy air travel around the globe.

In 1879 the great inventor Thomas Edison, after a number of attempts, created the light bulb, which has made life comfortable for us all. After his great achievement, Edison concentrated on creating a commercial application of the light bulb, and was able to sell the concept to homes and businesses by mass-producing relatively long-lasting light bulbs and creating a complete system for the generation and distribution of electricity.

All these achievements came about from dissatisfaction with the status quo and a desire for us all wanting more. They are a demonstration of an unlimited potential and growth that is within us all. We have unlimited learning capabilities. As human beings we are simply designed to grow and again. expand our talents and capabilities to suit our environmental needs and individual desires. Use these principles in your own life and build the life of your dreams.

The human mind is incredibly powerful, separating us from the animals we share this beautiful planet with. But we have something else too: our subconscious minds are connected to the great power of the universal mind, or what Carl Jung called the 'collective unconscious'.

These great powers of the mind allow us to tap into perfect solutions, but so many of us fail to use them. Only when we are struck down by extreme adversity do we discover our resilience and our great mental capabilities. For example, Milo C Jones owned a small farm in Wisconsin, USA on which he made a fair living. But in 1889, at the age of 35, he was struck down with arthritis, which paralysed every portion of his body with the exception of his brain. For most human beings this would mean the end of their life, but Milo Jones used the mental power of his mind and took control of it, most likely for the first time in his life. He discovered an idea that made him a small fortune and benefited him and his family and the lives of many other people. He had a vision of an idea of raising pigs and creating his own kind of sausages. It turned into a lucrative business, bringing him success and great wealth and changing his life for the better. He was able to live long enough to turn his vision into a reality and to enjoy the benefits of it, and this compensated him for the loss of his physical abilities.

Sometimes in life, only when we have been struck down by failure or defeat, do we discover and appreciate the true powers we possess from within. We discover our other self, the great power of our own mind.

The power of nature and gratitude

We live in an age in which life is so comfortable we can drive in a car, hop on a bus or a plane and go where we want to go. We can communicate and talk to anyone on this planet from the comfort of our car or our home, through modern technology. Society is built up on the creative power of different minds. Some of us may take for granted the great technological achievements that may have taken centuries to develop, but we would only know how marvellous it all is if it were gone.

Well, sometimes in life we do that with each other. So many times in life we take each other for granted. We get caught up in the busy day to day routine of life and we forget about friends and loved ones. We may have an elderly relative or a sick niece and we forget that time is not forever. We forget it, that is, until we receive the news, the news that a love one has passed away. I've experienced that in my life too many times. Nature has a tendency to take away what we neglect. If you neglect your health and wellbeing over time you may lose the health and wellness you once possessed, or if you neglect your work or your friends or relatives you may find that over time you lose them. This also applies to your own creative mind power. You lose what you don't use, through lack of appreciation. To create a beautiful garden you have to plant good seeds, you have to nurture and maintain it. But can you imagine what would happen if you failed to maintain that garden? Those beautiful seeds of abundance would then perish and die. The same applies to your own life.

> " This journey that we call life is a forever-changing dance of the laws of nature. "

It is so important in life to appreciate each other. It's so important in life to enjoy the people that make life special and worth living. To really appreciate the people in our lives, our loved ones, our family and friends, the people in our neighbourhood and at work, we must acknowledge them and appreciate them. Live your life in an attitude of gratitude and achieve the true riches that life has to offer you.

After watching your favourite film look at the credits, the list of names at the end, the actors and co-ordinators, the director, the producer, the makeup artist, the marketing company and the producer to name but a few. All these talented people came together to make that one film possible for us all to enjoy. All human beings are here to serve one another. You are serving someone in one way or another and someone is serving you. This is the human condition. We are all connected to make the good life we desire possible, and this constant act of giving is something to be truly grateful for.

When human beings come together and use the mastermind principles of joining great minds together as one, we can only achieve greatness that benefit us all. Now apply this principal to your own life and change your life for the better.

What we have learnt in this chapter...

- Gratitude allows you to see the good in your life and the good to come.

- This attitude allows you to feel happiness and joy which ads quality to your life.

- Happiness and joy in the mind improves health and general wellbeing.

- Ungrateful behavior leads to anger, sadness and hate.

- Negative emotional states produce lack of love, lack of friendships, lack of money and ill health.

- To turn your life around you must dig deep and see the riches in your life.

- A grateful attitude hooks you up to your source of supply, both in terms of success and love.

- When you are grateful for what you have, you will open yourself up to achieving and receiving more.

- Sometimes it is only when we have been struck down by failure or defeat that we discover and appreciate the true powers we possess from within. It is then that we discover our other self and the awesome power of our own mind.

Chapter 7
Prosperity consciousness

Prosperity consciousness

Prosperity consciousness is a powerful mindset that attracts to us all the riches that life has to offer. People who possess this way of thinking are focused only on opportunity. Their minds are fired up and dominated by the thoughts of success, constantly visualising big ideas, big dreams and a greater good to come to them. They see hope, they see freedom, happiness and joy, so they attract these things into their lives.

Remember that the human mind is the great power that pulls almost everything into your life. People with a poverty consciousness are simply misusing their mind power against themselves and creating a life that is filled with worries and fear. Poverty consciousness is like a bad programme in a sophisticated high powered computer, creating all the ills and disasters that human beings fear and don't want. Our ignorance and habitual ways of thinking allow us to continue in this way. We see the thoughts of lack and limitations; we constantly indulge in this practice of self-sabotage and wonder why this is happening to us again and again. We don't understand that it is our dominant programme that attracts these unwanted things into our lives. Change the programme and change your life for a better one!

Do you desire great freedom, happiness, wealth and prosperity? If you are thinking this way and have a strong desire to win, you are on your way to having a prosperity consciousness. Conversely, is your mind focused on lack and limitation? If your mind is focused on lack and limitation, don't you know that you are attracting more of this unwanted life style? You are attracting more of what you don't have. You would then have a poverty consciousness.

Most people talk about their problems over and over again every day but so often fail to spend time talking about solutions. They have a belief that the politicians and the government have the solutions to their troubles and forget about their own mind power, never realising that the answers lie in themselves. President John F Kennedy once said: "Ask not what your country can do for you, but what you can do for your country." He was right in that the answers lie in you. You hold the key to prosperity success and happiness in your life.

> "Prosperity thinking will make you see opportunity in almost every situation. This is a world of opportunity!"

With poverty consciousness your attention is focused on what you don't have. A person thinking this way will experience the feelings of not having enough. They see life as hard; they see a tough road ahead. Their eyes are closed to opportunities of wealth and success, and wealth and success is seen as only limited to the few. But the reality is that great wealth is available to any human being who desires it and is willing to have the right mindset to bring it into their lives.

With prosperity thinking you will see more opportunity than you ever imagined. See love, see joy, and see wealth and prosperity. You can achieve big things in life, if you believe in yourself and develop a prosperity consciousness. The only limitations are those you set for yourself. Every time you say I can't do this or that, I can't afford this, I can't afford that or I don't have enough of this, this becomes your reality. To obtain a prosperity consciousness you have to turn your thinking around. You have to see that there is enough love in your life, there is enough money and opportunity to earn more money; if you set your mind to achieve that it will become reality. You can change your life through a change of thought.

Right now there is a new job or career waiting for you. Money is available for you to buy the things you want and need. You are now in a position to help the people you love and cherish. Whatever you desire, it's out there waiting for you to call it into your life. You just have to open your eyes and your heart's desire and go and get it. Prosperity thinking will make you see opportunity in almost every situation. Now you see it's a world of opportunity. It's your world, your life. Understand there are no limitations in this world. There is an abundant supply of wealth and good health.

See the world as being a place of plenty, and this will be reflected in your own life. If it's a loving relationship you want, this will lead you to marriage and a loving home with children, a family of your own with people that love you and care for you. Your prosperity consciousness allows you to see this and feel the joy it brings even before it has actually happened. Maybe it's something you wanted for a long time. You can have all the love you desire, it's all here waiting for you to call it into your life by your prosperity thinking. You have the power to make it a reality and bring it into your life. If you believe in the love you have been waiting for, by the power of prosperity consciousness it is coming to you, because you called upon it. This mental awareness feeds directly to your subconscious mind and makes it happen. It may take some time but if you believe and have desire and passion for something it will come true.

> **"You hold the key to prosperity success and happiness in your life."**

You may not have love and financial wealth at the moment but you can change that by changing your thinking, otherwise you will continue to think there is no love and no money out there for you – and that is what you're going to get. Destroy the limitations of your current mindset. See the love and the financial wealth you desire and attract it into your life by developing a prosperity consciousness. So many times in life we focus on the things that get us down, we talk to family and friends about what we don't like and see it coming back into our lives time and time again. Focus on love, wealth and prosperity. When you think of the things you love and talk about the things you love you are calling to these things and that's what you will attract. You attract what you love. It is your human right to enjoy your life on this planet. Live your life.

The great Madam CJ Walker was an African-American woman, one of six children born into poverty in Delta Louisiana in 1867. She was an orphan at seven and worked in the cotton fields of Vicksburg with her young sister Louvenia. She survived abuse from a brother-in-law. But despite these hard knocks, plus losing a child, she became a strong woman. She had a strong will and a burning desire to create ideas that would improve her life and the lives of other people. In her vision she saw an opportunity to build and create her own destiny by developing and marketing a large successful line of beauty and hair products for black women by setting up the C.J. Walker Manufacturing Company. She became the first black female millionaire. Her famous words were: "I got my start by giving myself a start."

CJ Walker was SELFMADE. It doesn't matter where you are in life, it only matters where you are going and you can decide that by controlling your mind to see the opportunities and by creating your riches in life. You can do this by thinking prosperously and by the practice of visualising your success before it even happens, just like CJ Walker did.

> " With prosperity thinking you will see more opportunity than you ever imagined. See love, see joy, see wealth and prosperity. "

You may have a desire for more money and a more comfortable life, but this requires you to take the time to create ideas and products that people want and need – to learn new skills and abilities, including marketing and promotion. Your persistence in developing such products or services will itself be a source of your success. As human beings we are all here to serve each other. This is what makes the good life possible; if you are aware of it and want it badly enough you will achieve it. If you want more in life you must give more. Find ways to be of service, and in the process you will learn about yourself and your hidden talents, which you were given to use.

Prosperity consciousness and the law of polarity

For every up there is a down, for every right there is a left. For every back there's a front. There are some people winning, there are some people losing. An individual may see poverty and an individual may see prosperity. These are the laws of polarity that make up the human condition. Polarity means that there is always hidden potential in things – whether a thing seems good or bad just depends on how you see it. Don't let your negative mindset distort your thinking or cloud your judgment and rob you of your dreams, because such a mindset is not inherently 'real', it is just the way you are seeing it. Most people look at the rich and successful as aliens with super powers, and some people may fill up with envy. Envy can destroy a person's self-worth because they believe that it is not possible for them to achieve the same or even better. But if it is possible for them, then it is possible for you too.

In the 1930s, America suffered a Great Depression which brought hardship for millions of people. People lost their jobs and their lives. They saw no hope and no way out. It was inconceivable to even think of success in those conditions but even during these times there were people still winning. They included Henry Ford (Ford car motor company); Luther Burbank (scientist); John D. Rockefeller (entrepreneur); Andrew Carnegie (industrialist); and Napoleon Hill (writer and philosopher). Each of these people, through their thinking and achievements, was a light for others to follow. As Napoleon Hill said: "There are no limitations to the mind except those we acknowledge. Both poverty and riches are the offspring of thought."

What we have learnt in this chapter...

- Prosperity consciousness is a powerful mindset that attracts to us the enormous riches that life has to offer.

- People who possess this way of thinking are focused only on opportunity for success.

- The human mind is the great power that pulls almost everything into our life.

- People with a poverty consciousness are simply misusing their mind power against themselves and creating a life that is filled with worries and fear.

- You may not have love and financial wealth at the moment but you can change that by changing your thinking.

- If you persist in thinking that there is no love and no money for you then that is what you're going to get.

- You must destroy the limitations of your current mindset.

- See the love and the financial wealth you desire and attract it into your life by developing a prosperity consciousness.

Chapter 8
Self confidence
and its benefits

Self confidence and its benefits

S elf-confidence is the power of self-belief, or having a firm trust in your own abilities. This provides energy and drive to do the things you want to do. Your self-belief draws attention and excitement from others, making you a people magnet. Confidence is the characteristic of a winner, and this characteristic attracts success and power to individuals who possess it. Confidence, Donald Trump said, can get you where you want to go, and getting there is a daily process. Life and success is so much easier when you feel good about yourself, your abilities and talents.

Confidence makes things happen

Do you believe in yourself and your capabilities? We all have great mental facilities and capabilities beyond our own awareness. Take a look at your habits, and at the good and bad qualities you possess. What works and what's holding you back? Recognise the good, as this is what you will use to move you forward in your life. Be proud of the things that make you different from others! Good confidence is being comfortable within yourself. You know who you are, you know you are a good person, you are special, you have love in you and you care for your family and friends. You see the good in others and in yourself. You have no fear in expressing yourself and you have a healthy attitude about yourself and life and the people in it.

As Jamaican publisher, journalist and entrepreneur Marcus Garvey once said: "If you have no confidence in self, you are twice defeated in the race of life. With confidence, you have won even before you have started."

Do you appreciate yourself? How do you see yourself, your self worth; do you have a healthy love for yourself and well being? Do you have good will power and self belief? Sometimes we take ourselves for granted. We don't realise how important we are to others; we don't see the good that we do; we forget that we are a beautiful part of nature and we are put here to have an abundant life. Enjoy life – it's the most natural thing. We should feel alive, happy and ready to engage in our life on this planet.

Learn to be comfortable within yourself. A person should all be able to enjoy their own company, not feeling lonely when they are on their own. The fact that you enjoy your own company means others will enjoy your company too, as they can see the happiness in you.

Napoleon Hill said that the world has the habit of making room for the person whose words and actions show that he knows where he is going.

Your self-confidence is based on your belief in yourself. You believe in yourself and you have a healthy love for yourself. With this self love you will love others. You can only truly love other people when you have a healthy love for yourself. What is self love exactly? It is having an understanding of who you are and appreciating your qualities and seeing the good in yourself, appreciating that you are special. You know yourself; you're comfortable with your qualities and accept yourself for who you are. You're aware of your skills and capabilities and feel like you can take on the world. You are not afraid to take a chance on life. You have a desire to win and succeed in life and to improve and to achieve more. When you are truly comfortable within yourself you will find true happiness and you will see the good that life brings and people will want to be a part of you. The people in your life will pick up that positive energy that you possess and it makes them happy to be around you. A confident person is a positive, cheerful and happy human being who expresses the joy they feel from within.

When you love yourself you will love others too, you see the good in people, you see how beautiful the world is and you know you are a part of it. People enjoy your company and enjoy being around you, they can feel the good in your heart and it makes them feel good too. By giving more, you will achieve more, and with increased self esteem and confidence you will have the power to give more of yourself in whatever it is you do.

Self-belief and self-concepts shape your life

The great Henry Ford said: "Whether you think you can or think you can't, you are right." You are in control of your life and how you see it. Our beliefs and self-concepts shape our lives, including our decision making, our directions and choices we make in life. What you believe will be the way. What are your self beliefs. Your self-concepts and belief systems will determine the results in your life. Do you feel you are desirable? Do you see yourself as capable of achieving success? If you

> **" Learn to love your individual qualities as these are what make you special. "**

do, then that is what you will be. You see, your self-concept was formed when you were a child and paved the way for the life you have today.

Your self-concept from childhood is influenced by the people around you, your family, teachers and friends: how they interacted with you and what they may have said to you has a small vulnerable child. Your childhood holds a key to your current life situations and your current mind power and self-development. You may have experienced as a child or in your past some challenging times that made you believe you couldn't be successful in life. You may have felt hurt and discouraged. You may have shed tears of self-doubt, but you can now dry those tears and understand that you are special – maybe you just don't know it as yet.

So many of us go through life carrying a false image of ourselves due to our past experiences. So many people go through life believing that they are just an average person down the street, but that is so untrue –we are all unique. The average person really does not exist; we are all individuals with unique personalities and an individual outlook on life. The problem is that we fail to explore our individuality, choosing to conform to another individual's ideals of what is the so called norm, and then we fail to explore our talents and capabilities. We settle for what we don't want in life because of our own ignorance.

Some of us have talents and skills and abilities that we never use, and these capabilities could build a more productive and exciting life for us but we fail to use them; we have failed to unlock the genie in our higher selves. All human beings have greatness in them. It's there. We just have to find it and pull it out of our subconscious mind. A child may be labeled and judged by others and put down. People may give up on that child and this can have such a negative impact on a child's life and the direction they go. That's why a child's environment is so crucial in achieving success in their life, as this will determine whether a positive self concept or a negative self-concept is developed.

Regardless of what your past experiences in life may be, you can reprogramme your mind and build a positive life. In order for human beings to move forward they must override the inner demons of their past beliefs and understand anything in life is possible if they believe it

> " Whatever you decide to do,
> the power lies in you.
> You hold the key. "

is. True inner confidence is a person's inner beliefs of themselves and their capabilities. When you have fully opened your mind and changed your self-beliefs you will have given birth to genuine self-confidence

The great inventor, scientist and businessman Thomas Edison had a passion for creating things. It is said that he failed in inventing the light bulb a thousand times but still kept going until he achieved success

> " Confidence is the characteristic of a winner. This characteristic attracts success and power to the individuals who possess it. "

with a workable model. His will power and determination changed the world and our way of life. Edison had a vision that made him persist with his invention of the light bulb despite a thousand defeats. When asked by a reporter how he felt to have failed a thousand times, Edison simply replied that it took a thousand steps to get to his final, working invention. His ability to demonstrate extreme persistence led to his success, and if you use that idea of persistence and confidence you too can create successes in your life.

Edison is the third most prolific inventor in history, holding 1,093 US patents in his name, as well as many patents in the UK, France, and Germany. He is credited with numerous inventions that contributed to mass communication and, in particular, telecommunications. These include a stock ticker, a mechanical vote recorder, a battery for an electric car, electrical power, recorded music and motion pictures. His advanced work in these fields was an outgrowth of his early career as a telegraph operator. Edison originated the concept and implementation of electric-power generation and distribution to homes, businesses, and factories – a crucial development in the modern age. It was his creative vision, confidence and self-belief that led him to these historical

> **" Whether you think you can or think you can't, you are right. "**
> Henry Ford

inventions. He took control of his life and changed the world for the better. He was SELFMADE and you can be SELFMADE too.

The power of self-belief, vision, persistence and confidence changes lives and will show you the way to success. With the power of confidence and self-belief you will persist despite past failings. Keep the faith and win.

The power of confidence

Confidence gives you the will to believe in yourself and overcome challenging circumstances. Garrett Morgan (born in 1877) was an inventor and entrepreneur. At the age of fifteen he developed a skill as a handyman fixing and repairing things, and moved to Cincinnati, Ohio, in search of employment. Most of his teenage years were spent working as a handyman for a wealthy Cincinnati landowner. Like many African-Americans of his day, Morgan had to quit school at a young age to work. However, the teenaged Morgan was able to hire his own tutor and continued his studies while living in Cincinnati. In 1895, Morgan moved to Cleveland Ohio, where he worked repairing sewing machines for a clothing manufacturer.

Eight ways to transform negative beliefs

1. **Use positive affirmations** and feed positive self talk into your subconscious mind (see chapter 10 for more information about affirmations).

2. **Visualise yourself daily being happy and successful**. Any thoughts held in the mind will eventually be expressed in the physical world.

3. **Act like the successful person you want to be**. Visualise daily the new confident you and keep this image in your mind.

4. **Develop a prosperity consciousness** by focusing on opportunity and your good qualities.

5. **Love yourself** and change your-self beliefs

6. **Spend time with people who love you** and who believe in you and encourage you to properly express your greatness.

7. **Don't let negative thoughts or negative habits hold you back**. Sometimes the person looking at you in the mirror can be your own worst enemy. You must control your self-behavior and keep the inner demons at bay.

8. **You are SELFMADE**. Be the person you want to be in order to live the life of your dreams.

Your beliefs and self concepts pave the way we think and shape our lives. Repetition is the royal road to confidence. Doing something over and over again builds self-assurance and self-confidence in a human being. With the persistence and the power from within we begin to build the self-confidence that will propel us to the top of whatever it is we choose. Whatever it is you want, just do it and the confidence will come.

Word of his skill at fixing things and experimenting spread quickly throughout Cleveland, opening up various opportunities for him. In 1907, he opened his own sewing machine and shoe repair shop. It was the first of several businesses he would own. In 1908, Morgan helped found the Cleveland Association of African-American Men. His vision and confidence allowed him to grow from strength to strength in a time where it was thought there was a lack of opportunity for minority groups. In his early 30s, he expanded his business to include a tailoring shop. The company made coats, suits, dresses, and other clothing.

Morgan experimented with a liquid that gave sewing machine needles a high polish and prevented the needle from scorching fabric as it sewed. Accidentally, Morgan discovered that this liquid not only straightened fabric but also hair. He made the liquid into a cream and began the G.A. Morgan Hair Refining Company. Morgan also made a black hair oil dye and a curved-tooth iron comb in 1910, to straighten hair. Morgan was SELFMADE. He called the shots in his life and he set the goals and achieved them. You can take control of your life too, by creating goals and ideas, and combining persistence with experimentation.

What we have learnt in this chapter...

- Self confidence is the power of self belief.

- Confidence provides energy and drive which allows us to do the things we want to do.

- Your self belief draws attention and excitement from others.

- Confidence is the character of a WINNER!

- Feeling confident is being comfortable within yourself.

- Confidence is about knowing who you are… a special person, full of love that sees the good in others and in your self.

- When you are truly comfortable within yourself you will find true happiness.

- When you see the good that life brings, people will want to be a part of you!

- All of us have talents and skills and abilities that we never use, and these capabilities could build a more productive and exciting life for us but we fail to use them.

- All human beings have greatness in them – it is there, we just have to find it!

Chapter 9
Affirmations -
words of power

Affirmations - words of power

Affirmations are positive suggestions that you make to yourself to change the programme of your mind. They describe in positive words a desired situation you would like to come to pass. It could be an event or a goal. Their power lies in their repetition. These statements are repeated mentally or aloud. When these statements are repeated often with feelings and emotions they soon take root in our subconscious mind, and this then influences our behaviour in real life. It's like self hypnosis for success. They change the programming of your subconscious mind, which in turn transforms the way you think and behave. New opportunities are attracted into your life. What you repeatedly think and say with feeling and emotion is what you bring into your life.

What do you really desire? A better family life, more money, stronger health? Affirmations can help you! For instance, are you seeking to improve your self-confidence and self-esteem? Feed your mind with positive statements daily. By doing this you are reprogramming your mind for success and removing negative thoughts that are holding you back from the life you want and deserve.

Muhammad Ali once said: "It's the repetition of affirmations that leads to belief. And once that belief becomes a deep conviction, things begin to happen."

Your inner conversations, words, thoughts and feelings determine the kind of life and reality you experience. If you occupy your mind with negative thoughts and expect difficulties and problems, you will draw them into your life. If you constantly think success you will draw success in to your life. However, if you find it difficult to think positively, affirmations can help you change the way you think! They are a powerful method to transform your thinking patterns.

> " Affirmations are positive self-suggestions that you can make in order to change the programme of your mind. "

Overcoming negative self talk

Do you sometimes experience negative self talk? That little voice in your mind that says you can't do the things you desire. You have an idea, you have some sort of inspiration and you are just about ready to move into action - and then a voice in your mind says you can't do it. The voice continues to tell you you're not good enough, you're not cut out for it. This little voice continues with details of all the reasons that it's not possible for you to achieve your goals in life.

This little voice is formed from past experiences, sometimes negative childhood memories and sometimes from negative feedback from friends and relatives who mean well. Friends and relatives often judge

> # " The power of affirmations lies in their repetition. "

from their own limitations, but the damage is done and an individual can go through life believing that they are not deserving of achieving more out of life. This plague of negative talk destroys the lives of millions. So many people come into the world and go to the grave never fulfilling their true desires and dreams, simply because of their self beliefs and self concepts.

When you were born your mind was wide open, allowing all your influences and surroundings in to your subconscious mind (as we noted in Chapter 3:Changing habitual ways). These then form into negative thoughts and become a habit embedded into the subconscious mind. When the habit is challenged the negative self talk comes into play as a defence mechanism; this keeps an individual where they are. They may have a desire to move forward in life but the negative self talk can be so powerful it holds them back. Whenever this person tries to challenge the habit they are then plagued with fear and anxiety, which pushes them back into the so called comfort zone. The comfort zone is the zone of retreat. So much potential for happiness and success lies dead in the graveyard!

How can you overcome the power of negative self talk? Because the negative seed is so deeply buried in the subconscious mind, an individual doesn't even know it's there. This negative self talk reveals itself when you try to grow as a person. When you try to progress, suddenly you are bombarded with a thousand reasons why you can't do something that you would like to do. You are then forced into playing it safe and falling back into the comfort zone.

In order to overcome this condition that paralyses the genius in most people, negative self-talk must be removed and then replaced with a positive mindset. How can you form a positive mindset to propel you in the direction you want to go? You must feed the mind positive suggestions, positive affirmations - words of self-empowerment. For example, you may have been thinking for a long time that you cannot do something in particular, and you now replace those mental words with a statement of what you want to achieve.

> " Your inner conversations, words, thoughts and feelings determine the kind of life and reality you experience. "

You must continue to repeat and say empowering words. By persistence and a strong desire to succeed the old programme that has been holding you back will then fade away. This will then allow your new desired habits to take root, and they then become imbedded into your subconscious mind. Over time you will now find it easier to think positive. If you continue this behaviour it will then become a habit to naturally say positive affirmations in your mind. You will start to feel good. You will be the happier, cheerful, and achieving person as nature intended.

Here are some suggested affirmations:
- I am guided by the universal power to experience bliss every moment of my life.
- Love, happiness, health and wealth are my dominant thoughts.
- Peace, love, and harmony for me and my family and friends.
- I enjoy money, travel, wealth and prosperity and share this with others.
- I enjoy living in my lovely home.
- I have money and enjoy my financial security and can buy the things I want.
- My marvellous mind will direct me to peace and harmony with fruitful thoughts.
- The breath I inhale fills my body with strength and power.
- Thoughts of success and power dominate my mind and are my friends and companions.
- My mind is focused on my goal and I see it as an accomplished fact.
- I am a genius and I have creative powers that will improve my life and the lives of my loved ones.

Benefits achieved through affirmations

- Programme your subconscious mind for success.
- Attract money and abundance into your life for you and your family!

- Achieve your dreams and goals!
- Create positive and happy circumstances and situations!
- Get rid of negative habits and attitudes, and build positive ones instead!
- Surround yourself with positive people, like minded people!
- Boost your feelings of self confidence and inner strength!
- Motivate, energize and boost your inner strength!
- Improve your health and well being and enjoy more fun and happiness in life!

It's the repetition of information that will re-programme your mind to success. By following these principles you are on the road to reprogramming your subconscious mind.

Words are so powerful in their effect on feelings and emotions. Words can affect the moods of the mind. That's why affirmations are so effective. You will achieve what you feel you are capable of achieving, and feelings come from words spoken. In the past your limitations were self imposed, but you now understand that there are no limitations to what you can achieve. Feed your mind daily with positivity, as this is good for your mindset and overall health and well being. Positive affirmations are nutrition for the mind.

What we have learnt in this chapter...

- Affirmations are positive statements that describe in positive words our desires.

- Affirmations are like self hypnosis for success.

- When you repeat affirmations frequently and with passion, faith and emotion they change the programming of your subconscious mind.

- By changing your programming, you can transform the way you think!

- Your inner conversations, words, thoughts and feelings determine the kind of life and reality you experience.

- If you occupy your mind with negative thoughts and expect difficulties and problems, you will draw them into your life.

- If you constantly think of success you will draw success into your life.

- Positive affirmations are a powerful way to transform your thinking power.

Chapter 10
Love and relationships

Love and relationships

We all desire love. Love is that feeling of joy and oneness that we feel. Love is a connection, a connection to others. True love in a committed relationship can be so powerful that it dominates our lives and focus. The first love in a relationship is self-love. To bring happiness and joy into a relationship you must be happy within yourself, whereas a troubled mind breeds troubled relationships. It is so important for an individual to be honest with themselves and deal with any issues that are spoiling their ability to have an enjoyable relationship. So many times we look to our relationships to bring us happiness, not understanding that for the relationship to function well we have to deal with our own internal issues. If you are happy from within you will bring that warmth and happiness into the relationship. If you are not first happy from within nothing will fully make you happy.

With internal happiness we will be empowered to give more and we will receive more from our efforts. Focus on the giving and the rest will follow. You will enjoy good love, happiness, health and wealth. Personal development is a good way to improve your relationship because as you improve yourself everything in your life will improve too, including your relationship. Look for the good in your partner, observe and see their good qualities and compliment them verbally on what it is you like that they do. This positive approach will allow you to enjoy the good that they do and attract more of it. Don't wait for your partner to do something nice for you, take the initiative and make the first move, prepare a nice meal or a surprise that will make them smile.

Nothing can replace true love and happiness. You may have a beautiful home, a nice car and you may have an abundance of financial wealth but all of that is meaningless when you have no one to share it with; the true beauty of life is when we are able to share our riches with others. If you have just bought something nice to wear to a dinner date or a function of some kind, the pleasure comes from sharing it with others. Nothing can replace that powerful feeling we share with other human beings. The fuel of a relationship is giving to your partner, your friends and your life. What you put out is what you get back. If you have nothing and you want something then you have to create, you have to give and it will all turn around for you. Give love.

When beauty turns to pain

Sometimes in life we attract beauty that turns into bitterness and pain. We get involved in a relationship that first started out with joy and happiness, which can turn into abuse and pain. We have somehow attracted a negative person into our life. We all hear about abusive relations and it's hard for most people to understand why two people stay in a painful relationship. The main cause is our habits. The first attack of abuse could be seen as a one off encounter until it's repeated over and over again, and the constant repetition of this abusive behaviour gets planted into the subconscious mind of both parties involved in the relationship. Once implanted into the subconscious, the actions and thought patterns then manifest in the physical world, again and again. You now have the abused and the abuser locked into this painful habit of self-destruction. Where is the love you may ask? The love is still there but it is now buried deep, unable to express itself

> " True love in a committed relationship can be so powerful that it dominates our lives and focus. "

due to the over bearing pressures of the abusive habitual behaviour patterns in the relationship. These must be removed and replaced by new positive behaviour patterns, and this is not a walk in the park as it requires both parties to admit that there is first a problem and then come to terms with the fact that both involved are responsible. So often people allow undesirable emotions to fester inside, which eventually turn beauty into pain. In the world today there are literally millions of people living in unhappy relationships, going through their day to day lives in unhappiness, because they believe this is all that life has to bring them. On the outside it appears to be a beautiful relationship or a beautiful marriage, but behind closed doors these relationships are riddled with adultery, neglect, and physical and emotional abuse.

A loving relationship with happiness and joy is the stuff of life: we feel special, we feel wanted and alive. People may envy an individual enjoying such an experience of life, because you have what they truly desire and want. You see couples like this enjoying a loving relationship. They have happiness and bliss; a walk in the park, a quiet drive down country lanes, popping the top off a favourite bottle and cooking a romantic meal on a Sunday afternoon and enjoying intimate love.

But then comes the desire for us to explore and give into outside temptations. There are so many people in the world today living a lie, indulging in secret love affairs which may bring short term fulfilment and long term pain. This inner weakness that so many human beings suffer from destroys their family and their lives. A secret love affair is often self-destruction in disguise. Suddenly the love and attention from our partner or a good marriage is no longer enough. We give in to outside temptations from another, allowing the love and excitement we have to be destroyed. We bring shame to ourselves as we hurt our partner and our children or our family due our selfish acts. Why?

> " If you are happy from within you will bring that warmness and happiness into the relationship. "

All human beings carry the potential for self-destruction. That's why so many times in the media, in the newspapers and even in our everyday life you see a person who has it all, only to hear that they have done something illogical to destroy themselves. We wonder why they have taken those actions which bring them nothing more than disgrace and pain. It's almost as if, when we achieve our goals in life we have nowhere to go, so we bring ourselves back down to earth from that cloud of success by indulging in self-destructive behaviour, when we should really be chasing bigger goals to keep our happiness and success consistent.

" Focus on the giving and the rest will follow. "

Our true challenges for happiness come from within ourselves. We may give into temptation to indulge in unwanted meaningless intimacy behind our loving partner's back. We may indulge in over excessive drinking and smoking, we may over eat for comfort, and we may abuse and destroy a potentially good relationship or marriage... Why? No one is perfect, but the purpose of this book is to encourage you to achieve personal excellence and to improve the success in your life. Make it a habit to grow and improve the love in your life as much you do with other goals, and only then will you find true, long lasting relationships.

Appreciate what you have, and if you feel dissatisfied at times, make yourself bigger than this. You are a creative being so create ideas that will improve your relationship; be charming and exciting and keep the love alive. Don't allow yourself to be vulnerable in searching for happiness. Understand that one night of passion can be a lifetime of pain. Keep calm and find the inner happiness inside. Give love and you will receive love and enjoy the love inside. Enjoy the love you have found and stay happy as happiness begins inside. Think honesty and fidelity to your partner. Use the power of visualisation, use the power of affirmations, think and feel love, joy and happiness and attract love joy and happiness into your life. By the power of wisdom and faith, it is possible.

What we have learnt in this chapter...

- The first love in a relationship is self love.

- To bring happiness and joy into a relationship you must be happy within yourself.

- A troubled mind breeds troubled relationships.

- Nothing can replace true love and happiness.

- You may have a beautiful home, a nice car and you may have an abundance of financial wealth but all of this is meaningless when you have no one to share it with.

- The true beauty of life is when we can share our riches with others.

- Appreciate what you have, and if you feel dissatisfied at times make yourself bigger than this, you are a creative being, so create ideas that will improve your relationship.

- Be charming and exciting and keep the love alive.

- A loving relationship with happiness and joy is the stuff of life. We feel special, we feel wanted and alive. This is the way a human being should feel and was born to be.

Chapter 11
Meditation
and its benefits

Meditation and its benefits

Do you want peace of mind? Do you sometimes feel stressed out by problems, worries and fear? Perhaps your body feels tired and worn out with the tremors and vibrations of fear, or perhaps you can't stop the inner chatter of your mind, which plagues you with negative thoughts and anxiety.

These mental states make us feel angry and argumentative, because we have only negative feelings and emotions and pain inside of us. We have nowhere to put that unhappiness we feel, and often we will take it out on our loved ones. This obviously has a bad affect on our relationships and lives. We live in a constantly busy and stressful world, with so much going on. When do we ever get the chance or the time to relax for that inner peace and joy that is a natural part of us? So many of us look for external forces for our solutions which may help in the short term, but don't bring us long term happiness and joy. We need to be comfortable from within ourselves; we can never find real happiness and joy until we are happy and comfortable from within – for there is the real joy.

How do we get there? How do we find that inner peace and joy to take us away from the constant inner chatter of our mind or external events? All human beings must find the time to slow down. It is so vital to put the brakes on and take stock of our lives to avoid the overload of stress that a fast pace society brings.

We need to find a way to calm the mind down and take control of it: to feel the true joy of that inner power that all human beings have. Through contemplation and relaxation we can achieve a state of calmness of mind. When you can silence the inner chatter of your mind you are at the true core of your being. The spirit and the soul that you are, that is the real you. You are not your mind. The mind is simply your guide that connects you to the Creator, a guide that we depend on and use, but in order to use our minds effectively we must take control of it. By silencing the mind, this will allow us to be more focused and alert, and at the same time enable our natural creativity and intuition to come to the surface. When used correctly the mind is like a genie – it can bring you what you want in this life. Some tips for achieving a calm mind:

1. Listen to peaceful relaxation music
2. Go for a walk
3. Control your breathing and thinking
4. Meditate regularly

The power of meditation

Some of us make a choice to start thinking positive about life. We read the books, listen to the CDs, go to the seminars. We're feeling good and positive - and then it happens: one by one the negative thoughts start to reappear in our minds, taking control of our thoughts and thinking. These negative thoughts can create self-doubt and lack of confidence, and of course worry and fear.

Don't you wish you could just switch it off? Switch off the inner chatter of your mind which says things like : Ive got that bill to pay, I don't want to be late, I bet my partner doesn't love me - all the thoughts that can destroy your happiness. But through meditation you switch off this negative chatter and allow your mind to relax. This relaxation brings peace and harmony to your entire being. You feel relaxation in your mind and body.   Meditation is a practice to empty the mind of thoughts in order to concentrate and control its power, also giving you more control over your thoughts and feelings. You can now control your mind to visualise your goals and create new ideas to improve your life, and you then feel more creative and can think of solutions to challenging problems. By detoxing your mind of negative thinking, suddenly harmony and peace is restored into your life.

History of meditation

Meditation goes back thousands of years.   It is thought that it was discovered by ancient warriors staring into the flames of their fires; this focused their minds and allowed them to experience altered state of consciousness. Over time, meditation evolved into a structured practice. Indian scriptures called Tantras mentioned meditation techniques over 5,000 years ago. The Buddha first made his mark around 5000 years BC, then his teachings spread through Asia.

The techniques of meditation came to the West in the 20th century, and in the 1960s and 1970s many professors and researchers started to try meditation practices. Today meditation is now popularly used in the West and worldwide. It is recognised by many as a good way to overcome a stressful life style, and an effective way to overcome or avoid depression and anxiety altogether.

Yet meditation is not just a practice, it can be a way of life that detoxes the mind from negative harmful thoughts, improving and enhancing the quality of your life by relieving you of stress. Stress is one of the major causes of ill health and a short life, so meditation has become a way of life for many – including the rich and famous – for good reasons.

> " Meditation can bring you the inner peace that you have always longed for and will improve the quality of your life. "

In the 1960s, the singer Tina Turner used meditation techniques to overcome a stressful relationship and the fast paced life style of a rock star. It helped her reinvent herself and propelled herself to the top of her field. Tina Turner was SELFMADE, and you too can remake yourself through meditation and have a stress-free lifestyle.

The actor and activist Richard Gere also made meditation a way of life. Apart from his fame as a film actor, Gere is a passionate advocate for human rights in Tibet; he is a co-founder of Tibet House, has created the Gere Foundation and is also the Chairman of the Board of Directors for the International Campaign for Tibet.

The jazz musician Herbbie Hancock, is another who knows the benefits of meditation. He is a longstanding practitioner of Nichiren Buddhism, which has a heavy emphasis on chanting as a form of meditation. Hancock is a member of the Japanese Buddhist movement, Soka Gakkai International, of which Tina Turner is also a member. These celebrities and many more have made meditation as a way of life. There are of course many forms of meditation, and you must choose which one is right for you to bring you to a state of inner peace and happiness.

The principles of meditation

1. The practice of meditation requires concentration. In order for us to concentrate, we need to focus on our mind one object at a time.
2. As soon as our thoughts start to wander, we slowly bring them back to the object that we are focusing on.
3. We try to ignore all distractions or irrelevant thoughts and sensations that our body may feel, or let them just pass like clouds in the sky.

The benefits of long term meditation

Meditation can bring you the inner peace that you have always longed for, and will improve the quality of your life. Meditation will allow you to block out those negative thoughts and suggestions that have been holding you back for years. You will find it easier to focus your mind and think rationally, and come up with new ideas and solutions that will

> " Through contemplation and relaxation we can achieve a state of calmness of mind. "

help you solve problems that have been getting you down. When you are feeling this calmness you will become more creative and see the world in a different way; you see the windows of opportunity that have always been there for you. This new way of living will make it easier to deal with life's challenges.

The benefits include:
• Peace of mind and self-confidence
• Reduced stress levels
• Improved health and well being
• Control over your mind and thoughts
• Detachment and inner peace
• Happiness and joy and a feeling of freedom
• Improved concentration and focus
• Increased spontaneity and creativity
• Powerful concentration
• An awareness of the purpose of life and a love for humanity and nature

Use these benefits wisely and create and achieve the things you want in life. The most important thing is that these techniques will make you feel good. You will feel peace and you will feel energised as your mind becomes free from all the stress, the worries and anxiety that have been distorting your inner power. You are now free to build and create the life that you want. You will be able to enjoy a good life with your family and friends, a more loving relationship and quality time with your partner. All of this is possible when a human being feels comfortable from within. This is the great power of calmness of mind.

> " When you can silence the inner chatter of your mind you are at the true core of your being. "

In 1899, Mahatma Ghandi proved himself more powerful than the British army by using the technique of satyrgraha, or non-violence. This is a demonstration of how effective a calm mind can be. It might seem a paradox to say this, but you can win the battle of modern day life simply by having a calm and happy mind.

The philosopher James Allen observed that man is made or unmade by himself because he is the master of his thoughts. Man holds the key to every situation and contains within himself the transforming and regenerating agency by which he may make himself what he wills.

All human beings are creators. We have a powerful mind, which has highly developed faculties that are connected to the creator of all things, and only when we take control over this glorious power and use it to our benefit can we enjoy the true beauty of life.

What we have learnt in this chapter...

- Meditation is a good way to overcome a stressful lifestyle as it detoxes the mind.

- Meditation is an effective way to overcome or avoid depression and anxiety altogether.

- Meditation can bring you the inner peace that you have always longed for and will improve the quality of your life.

- Meditation will allow you to block out negative thoughts and suggestions that have been holding you back for years.

- Through the practice of meditation, you will find it easier to focus your mind and think rationally.

- With meditation you will be able to come up with new ideas and solutions that will help you solve problems that have been getting you down.

- When you are feeling calmness you will become more creative and see the world in a different way. You see the windows of opportunity that have always been there for you.

- Mediation provides PEACE OF MIND!!

- This new way of living will make it easier to deal with life's challenges.

Chapter 12
What we've learned

What we've learned

Every human being wants something out of life. We are born creators with powerful imaginations. We have the ability to create ideas and we have the power to execute those ideas. We have developed the ability to imagine and create going back to childhood days when we thought about what we would like to be when we grow up.

A person who is SELFMADE is simply one who deliberately thinks about who they want to be and what they want to achieve and then takes the necessary actions to bring those ideas to life. Such a person is not 'going along with the flow'; their life is carefully thought out and planned. They have direction and purpose. If they need advice they speak to the right person. If it's further education they need, they do what is required to get the education. Without compromising the rights of others, they do what it takes to achieve their success in life. They have a plan, they have a vision, they have a goal and they put the plan into action and change their lives for the better.

Remember that you are at all times working with a power: your mind, your thoughts and feelings. Your thoughts and feelings will at all times affect your life. Because you are a being of power, you can change the image you have of yourself. Be careful to be feeling the best level of emotion possible at any one moment, and your life will reflect this elevated state. Sometimes you will come across people who will tell you you're not good enough, you're not smart enough. You must over ride that negative talk and stay true to yourself and your newfound positive attitude and persist in achieving your goals and dreams. On your journey you will find out what works for you and you will find the answers to take you where you want to go.

At some points you may blame 'bad luck', when in fact all you need is a goal, a purpose, or a vision to take control of your life and move in the direction you want. A goal has power that allows a human being to find their true self. A goal gives a human being a reason to live and a purpose to exist.

> " Goals give you a reason to live and a purpose to exist. "

Write down your goals and dreams and visualise them every day. Visualise your goals as though they have already happened. Visualise the things you want in life, your hopes and dreams and attract them into your world. Take time to sit down and think of the great life you want, think how it would be. Happiness is a natural part of our being. It's important to feel good from within. Quote affirmations that will reprogramme your subconscious mind and unlock the key to your happiness, wealth and success.

Be persistent in your goals. You may face tough challenges at times in pursuing them – this is natural and all successful people face challenges. It is part of the price you must pay in order to achieve success. No matter how many times you may have failed, don't give up.

Remember, you only need to win once in order to change your life forever.

Don't spend time thinking of why you can't achieve, spend time thinking of why you can. Sit down and think of big ideas that are going to change your life and will also improve your life and the loved ones you care about. Don't be discouraged or distracted by others, think and find the genius in you and create new ideas that will improve the quality of your life.

Through this book you have the formula that you need to change your life and give you what you want. But it will only work if you use it persistently.

> " Ensure you feel the best level of emotion possible at any one moment and your life will reflect this elevated state."

If you have a desire, a dream a passion and you want more out of your life, don't turn away in fear. Your dream can come true from your belief and your actions. Do you really want to change your life for the better? If you are serious, read the book again until its ideas and illustrations become part of your mind and start creating habits. Gradually these habits will influence your actions and change your life for the better.

> " On your journey you will find out what works for you and you will find the answers to take you where you want to go. "

The behaviour patterns and actions I've suggested are universal and can be used to improve your career and personal life without compromising the rights of others. Don't give up on your dreams. All the successful people who have achieved great happiness, wealth and success in life have used the ideas in this book, whether consciously or unconsciously.

You now have the knowledge for achieving your goals and dreams. You have learned about the purpose of goals, you understand visualisation, which means you have seen your dreams in your mind; you are now grateful for what you have and are aware of what you can achieve. You now know that what you currently have is the foundation for what you will have in the future. These are the building blocks of your success. You are now open to positive thinking and are aware of the opportunities to achieve your true purpose in life. You know who you are and that you can become self-confident. You can enjoy and see the beauty in the world and know you are a part of it; it's your world. So many of us go through life never being the person we want to be. You only have one shot as the person you are and as far as we know you don't get a second chance. Use your time wisely and go for your dreams. Be SELFMADE.

> # " Decide right now that you are going to change your life. "

A baby takes its first steps, then tumbles and falls. The baby keeps trying until they can walk and run and then jump. You may tumble, you may fall, but one day you will jump. That day is today.

There so many things that you can do, you may have not explored them as yet. We can be who we want to be if it is our desire. A nurse can become a singer and a song writer if that is her wish. A mother with three kids can turn her life in a new direction and start her own company if that is her strong desire. A man sleeping rough on the streets in the inner cities can find his inner strength and reinvent himself and change his life for the better. An administrator can become a philosopher and a writer can become a public speaker. You no longer need to limit yourself, to put yourself in a box. Be bold, be the individual you were born to be. So many of us go through life following the crowd, never finding our true self. Overcome your negative habits and outside influences that have been holding you back for so many years and make a decision right now that you are going to change your life.

You can create a life that's worthy of you and your family: the people you love and care about. You have the capabilities and the mental faculties to do or be who you want to be. You can take action and live out your dreams and turn those dreams into a reality. It's in your hands. You are SELFMADE.

What we have learnt in this chapter...

- A person who is SELFMADE is simply one who deliberately thinks about who they want to be and what they want to achieve and then takes the necessary action to make it happen.

- With your new positive outlook you will find the answers to enable you to live the life you want.

- Sometimes you may blame set backs or failure on bad luck. However, all you need is a goal, a purpose in life and a vision to allow you to take control of your life and achieve HAPPINESS!

- Write down your goals and dreams and visualize them every day.

- Visualize your goals as though they have already arrived.

- Visualise the things you want in life, your hopes and dreams and attract them into your world.

- Use strong powerful affirmations as suggested in this book.

- Remember you are a wonderful human being. Have faith and reprogram your subconscious mind in order to build a life that's worthy of YOU!

Author's note

For the past three years I have spent virtually every day studying the philosophy of personal development. When I read my first book in this area, I discovered a power that I didn't know existed. I have studied authors and philosophers dating back over a hundred years, but in fact the philosophy in this book goes back more than a thousand years, and contains a secret that only a few have fully realised. In his recording The Strangest Secret, Earl Nightingale noted that it was a strange secret because in one way it was so obvious, and yet for some reason it remained hidden that people didn't know they possessed a great power - that is, their own mind. This is simply because society conditions us to survive on our five senses, ignoring the ever potent power within. This is a faculty that all human beings have, but are taught from childhood not to use. If people do use it, they usually don't know that they are working with a great power - a power that is inside them, that is connected to the universal power: the universal mind... the power of creation...the power of God.

In the 1930s, the author Napoleon Hill revealed the power in his book *Think and Grow Rich*. Hill researched more than five hundred of the world's most successful people and discovered a golden thread that they all possessed. In 1902, the English author James Allen wrote a book on this power called As A Man Thinketh. This book influenced many later contemporary writers including Norman Vincent Peale, Earl Nightingale, Denis Waitley and Tony Robbins, among others. Yet they were only re-expressing a philosophy that has been around for centuries.

I am now passing this knowledge on to you so that you will use it to create and discover a life that's worthy of you. I know that we are all conditioned to read a book once or watch a film once and feel 'yes', this is now going to change my life. If you really want to change your life, however, you will need to read this book more than once and take these ideas further so that you have programmed your subconscious mind and made them into a habit. You will then get the results that you desire. You may know the knowledge on a conscious level, but in order to use the power of the subconscious mind, which is your greatest power, you need to study the book repeatedly. You will then change and your life will change for the better. You will be SELFMADE.

I want to give thanks to God for making it possible for me to communicate this philosophy and create this book. I want to thank my Mum and Dad for supporting me and encouraging me for more than twelve months of writing, and also my family and friends. Also thanks to Tom Butler-Bowdon for editing my work and adding that extra magic to bring SELFMADE alive. Many thanks to all who have made it possible. Thank you.

NOW, THE BEGINNING OF YOUR LIFE!

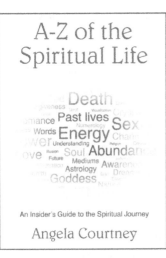

A-Z of the
Spiritual Life

An insider's guide to
the spiritual journey

by Angela Courtney

Available from Amazon and
www.liveitpublishing.com

What might you experience
when living a spiritual life?

What secrets are there to discover?

If you need answers to the big
questions then this book can help.

Describing the author's experience of spirituality over the last 20 years it is packed with valuable advice, stories and observations of a life created from the inside out.

Written in a lively but reassuring style the book is a series of postcards on everything from Power to Past Lives, Sex to the Sub Conscious. Including many unique descriptions of spiritual experiences such as:

- How it feels to connect with your Higher Self
- How change is instant when you stop sacrificing what you want
- How Love comes to us when we meditate
- Understanding how relationships are our guide and what to do about it
- How we create everything in our lives including world events

Lightning Source UK Ltd.
Milton Keynes UK
UKOW06f2329140916

283033UK00020B/502/P